Praise for *Oppositions*:

'Gaitskill's intuition ... borders on clairvoyance. Her prescience is agenda-free, but it's her exceptionally discerning writings on women ... that make one wish she had (or even wanted) her own syndicated newspaper column'

Kate Bolick, *New York Times Book Review*

'As in her fiction, Gaitskill sees everything ... [These] essays further establish her as the important critical thinker she's always been. Her extreme sensitivity makes her one of the most reliable witnesses to life in the US'

Chris Kraus, *4Columns*

'Gaitskill uses compassion as a conduit for interpretation'

Larissa Pham, *Nation*

'Gaitskill has a gift for traversing taboo territory with a subtlety that's sometimes downright Jamesian ... She draws on her personal experience to crack the veneers of the social codes and sexual ambiguities we all navigate'

Boston Globe

'Mary Gaitskill never fails to transport her reader ... These essays not only embrace but define their subjects, making you rethink the way you interact with the things around you in a much more meaningful way'

Newsweek

'Expect to never look at any of her subjects the same way again'

Cosmopolitan

'A beautiful, thought-provoking work that cements Mary Gaitskill as one of the sharpest critical thinkers and most important cultural critics of our time'

Bustle

'[Mary Gaitskill] says the things you didn't know needed to be said until she says them, and only then do you know what you've been missing'

Buffalo News

'Immersing yourself in [Gaitskill's] world for a page or three has the bracing aliveness of throwing yourself into almost-freezing water'

Columbus Dispatch

'Mary writes with startling, otherworldly clarity, peeling back the surface of things we might think we understand to peer into the slippery psychological realities underneath'

Big Think

'Gaitskill's biting tongue and literary pyrotechnics make for a delightful combination'

Booklist

'This collection of essays spanning two decades has the same fearless curiosity about the human psyche that Gaitskill exhibits in her fiction, along with the same unerring precision of prose ... The pages burst with insight and a candid, unflinching self-assessment'

Publisher's Weekly (starred review)

OPPOSITIONS

SELECTED ESSAYS

ALSO BY MARY GAITSKILL

The Mare
Don't Cry
This is Pleasure
Veronica
Because They Wanted To
Two Girls, Fat and Thin
Bad Behavior
Lost Cat: A Memoir
Da Capo Best Music Writing 2006 (editor)

OPPOSITIONS

SELECTED ESSAYS

MARY GAITSKILL

First published in Great Britain in 2021 by Serpent's Tail,
an imprint of PROFILE BOOKS LTD
29 Cloth Fair
London
EC1A 7JQ
www.serpentstail.com

A different version of this collection was first published in the United States of America
by Pantheon Books, a division of Penguin Random House LLC, in 2017 under the title
Somebody with a Little Hammer

10 9 8 7 6 5 4 3 2 1

Typset in Freight Text by MacGuru Ltd
Designed by Barneby Ltd
Printed and bound in Great Britain by Clays Ltd, Elcograf S.p.A.

A CIP record for this book can be obtained from the British Library

ISBN: 978 1 78816 815 1
eISBN: 978 1 78283 857 9

Contents

READING

OPPOSITIONS
SELECTED ESSAYS

Living

A Lot of Exploding Heads: On Reading the Book of Revelation

I did not have a religious upbringing and for most of my life I've considered that a good thing; I've since come to know people who felt nurtured by their religious families, but for a long time, for me, "religious upbringing," meant the two little girls I once walked home with in the fourth grade who, on hearing that I didn't believe that Jesus was the Son of God, began screaming, "There's a sin on your soul! You're going to Hell!" It meant my friend who, as a kid, was repeatedly exorcised in her mother's fundamentalist church and who still had nightmares about it at forty-five. It meant a thirteen-year-old boy who once told me he believed that God would punish his sexually active classmates by giving them AIDS. When I watched *The Exorcist* in theaters when it first came out and saw adult moviegoers jump up and stumble toward the exits, retching and/or weeping with fear, it was to me yet another bad example of what religious upbringing could do.

My mother, to her credit, told me that "God is love" and that there is no hell. But I don't think I believed her. Even though I have very little conscious religious anxiety, since childhood, I have had dreams that suggest otherwise; dreams of hooded monks carrying huge, grim crosses in processions meant to end

3

in someone's death by fire, drowning or quartering; of endless liturgies by faceless choirs to faceless parishioners in cavernous dark churches; of trials, condemnations, sacrifices, and torture; when I wake from these dreams it is with terror. Such things *have* actually occurred, but I still have no idea why they are so deeply present in me. Horror movies and creeping cultural fear are obvious sources, but my unconscious has taken these images in with such kinetic intensity and conviction that suggestion and vague historical knowledge don't seem to have been the cause.

When I was twenty-one, I became a born-again Christian. It was a random and desperate choice; I had dropped out of high school and left home at sixteen, and while I'd had some fun, by twenty-one, things were looking squalid and stupid. My boyfriend had dumped me and I was living in a rooming house and selling hideous rhodium jewelry on the street in Toronto, which is where the "Jesus freaks" approached me. I had been solicited by these people before and usually gave them short shrift, but on that particular evening I was at a low ebb. They told me that if I let Jesus into my heart right there, even if I just said the words, that everything would be okay. I said, all right, I'll try it. They praised God and moved on.

Even though my conversion was pretty desultory, I decided to pray that night. I had never seriously prayed before, and all my pent-up desperation and fear made it an act of furious psychic propulsion that lasted almost an hour. It was a very private experience that I would find hard to describe; suffice to say that I felt I was being listened to. I started going to a bleak church that had night services and free meals, and was attended heavily by street people and kids with a feverish, dislocated look in their eyes. And, for the first time, I started reading the Bible. For me, it was like running into a brick wall.

I was used to reading, but most of it was pretty trashy. Even when it wasn't, the supple, sometimes convoluted play of modern

4

language entered and exited my mind like radio music—then, of course, there was the actual radio music, the traffic noise, the continual onrush of strangers through the streets I worked, the slower shifting movements of friends, lovers, alliances, the jabber of electricity and neon in the night. All of which kept my mind and nervous system in a whipsawed condition from which it was difficult to relate to the Bible. *The earth was without form and void; and darkness was on the face of the deep. And the Spirit of God was hovering over the face of the waters. Then God said let there be light and there was light.* I couldn't even appreciate the beauty of the words. The phrases seemed like big dumb swatches of form imposed on something swift-moving and endlessly changeable. The form was mute, huge, and absolutely immobile. It made me feel I was being smothered. One clergyman after another would quote from it so intensely, as if its big, majestic opacity was meaningful in and of itself, and I would try to at least feel the meaning if I couldn't comprehend it. But all I felt was that persistent sense of truncation, the intimation of something enormous and inchoate trying to squeeze through the static form of written words.

This feeling became most intense when I read the Revelation. Next to Job, the Revelation is the most cinematic and surreal part of the Bible—it's a little like a horror movie, which is probably why it was relatively easy for a modern teenager to take in: there's a lot of explosions. It seemed terribly real to me; I would walk out into the streets, amid the big buildings in which commerce ground forward, and I would feel the violence, the lies, the grotesque pride, the *filth*, pitching and heaving under the semblance of order. The air would crackle with the unacknowledged brutality of life, and I would feel acutely all the small, stupid betrayals I committed daily, both against myself and others. The angels with their seven stars and their lamps, the beast with his seven heads and ten horns—the static imagery was sinister and senseless to me, and yet all the more convincing for it. I could imagine

5

angels and beasts looming all about us, incomprehensible and invisible to our senses the way the images in a photograph would be incomprehensible and invisible to a cat. Their stars and lamps and horns seemed like peculiar metaphors on the page, but, I feared, when the divine horses came down, with their fire and teeth and snake tails, their reality would be all too clear. I lay in my bed and prayed, trying to convince myself of God's love, but my prayers seemed a rag in a typhoon.

Besides, I couldn't help but think it was awfully harsh. Malignant sores, scorpions, fire, men "gnawing their tongues" with pain—I knew people were horrible, but even in my youth I could also see that most people did the best they could. Even as angry and fearful and disappointed as I was, I knew I wouldn't torture people like that, and I didn't see how I could be kinder than God. I was moved when I read, in First Corinthians 13: *Love suffers long and is kind; love does not envy; love does not parade itself, is not puffed up; does not behave rudely, does not seek its own, is not provoked, thinks no evil, does not rejoice in iniquity, but rejoices in truth; bears all things, believes all things, hopes all things, endures all things. Love never fails.* But I also remember thinking, and love is not pathologically cruel, either.

The rage of Revelation sometimes made my compassion feel weak and mealy-mouthed, but my reservations were not only humanitarian. I was more perturbed by what to me was the mechanical quality, not just of Revelation, but of the whole Bible. You had to worship God in exactly a certain way, according to certain prescriptions—and Revelation hinted that the rules set out in, say, the Ten Commandments, were only one tiny piece of a vast schema in which human ambivalence was simply not a factor.

*

During this time I had a dream which was not about the Bible, but which embodied my consternation about it. In the dream I lived in a house with several other people. We could not get out of the house and our relationships with each other had been pre-ordained, regardless of feeling. Our actions were controlled by a master whom we never saw. One day a man came to visit us, ostensibly for lunch. He was very polite and even friendly, and we were also friendly with him. But it was understood that he was one of the people who controlled us, and the atmosphere was one of pure dread. During lunch, when one of the men of the house seized and killed one of the household cats, we knew it was because our visitor had somehow made him do it. I couldn't hide my horror completely and our visitor looked at me a moment and then said, referring to the mangled body of the cat, "That's what I'm going to do to you one day." I understood him to mean that he was going to rape me, and I said "But I'm married," not because it mattered to me, but because I knew that the only thing that mattered to him was his laws, including the law of marriage. Then I became too angry to go along with this and I added, "Even though I don't respect my husband." Very threateningly—after all, it's part of the law that we love our spouses—the visitor asked, "Do you have sex with your husband?" I answered yes, and it was clear from my tone that I did so in order to obey the law. "That's good," said the visitor, "because your husband is a very intelligent man." Even for a dream, this was a strange moment: there was such a sense of approval for the fact of my husband's intelligence, but it had nothing to do with the man he was; rather the approval was all for the idea of an intelligent man and a dutiful wife paying him the homage of sex. The hellish thing was, within the dream, it was true. Even though I didn't love my husband, I considered him intelligent. And so I said, "Yes, he is very intelligent." I said it for complicated reasons. Partly to please the visitor, whom I was afraid of, but more to make some emotional contact with him by

7

invoking a concept he had codified as law, and making him see that I respected intelligence too. The way he looked at me when I said this was also complicated. It was a look of respect for my miserable loyalty to my husband, for my detached admiration for his mind. It was a look that appreciated my humanity, but would only give it a tiny space to live, a look a torturer might give a victim who had just expressed a sentiment the torturer considered noble, but that would not prevent the torture from taking place.

The prison-house of this dream seemed to me to be a metaphor for our human state, the circumstances of our birth into families not of our choosing, and our inability to free ourselves from a psychological make-up learned before we can decide for ourselves what we want to be. The visitor seemed like the God in the Bible who is kind only as long as you adhere to the rules, and who will sometimes decide to punish you anyway. God famously doesn't afflict Job because of anything Job has done, but because he wants to prove a point to Satan.

*

Twenty years later, I am sympathetic with my first assessment; to me, in spite of the soft, radiant beauty of many of its passages, the Bible still has a mechanical quality, a refusal to brook complexity that feels brutal and violent. There has been a change, however. When I look at Revelation now, it still seems frightening and impenetrable, and it still suggests an inexorable, ridiculous order that is unknowable by us, in which our earthly concerns matter very little. However, it no longer reads to me like a chronicle of arbitrarily inflicted cruelty. It reads like a terrible abstract of how we violate ourselves and others and thus bring down endless suffering on earth. When I read *And they blasphemed God of heaven because of their pain and their sores and did not repent of their deeds,* I think of myself and others I've known or know who blaspheme life itself by failing to have the courage to be honest and kind—and how then we rage around and lash out because we hurt. When I read "fornication," I don't read it as a description of sex outside legal marriage: I read it as sex done in a state of psychic disintegration, with no awareness of one's self or one's partner, let alone any sense of honor or even real playfulness. I still don't know what to make of much of it, but I'm inclined to read it as a writer's primitive attempt to give form to his moral urgency, to create a structure that could contain and give ballast to the most desperate human confusion.

I'm not sure how to account for this change. I think it mainly has to do with gradually maturing and becoming more deeply aware of my own mechanicalness and my own stringent limitations when it comes to giving form to impossible complexity—something writers understand very well. It probably has to do with my admittedly dim understanding of how apparently absolute statements can contain enormous meaning and nuance without losing their essential truth. And it has to do with my expanded ability to accept my own fear, and to forgive myself for my own mechanical responses to things I don't understand. In the past, my compassion was small—perhaps immature is a better word—and conditional. I could not accept what I read in the Biblical book because I could feel the truth of it in my own psyche. Now I recognize, with pain, a genuine description of how hellish life can be, and that it is not God who "sent" us to this hell.

To me, these realizations don't mean I have arrived at a point of any real knowledge, but they are interesting as markers of my development. I imagine that twenty years from now, when and if I read Revelation I will once again see it the same, but differently. I will look forward to it.

1994

The Trouble with Following the Rules: On "Date Rape," "Victim Culture" and Personal Responsibility

In the early 1970s I had an experience that could be described as "date rape," even if it didn't happen when I was on a date. I was sixteen and staying in the apartment of a slightly older girl I'd just met in a seedy community center in Detroit where I was just passing through. I'd been in her apartment for a few days when an older guy (he was probably in his mid-twenties) came over and asked us if we wanted to drop some acid. In those years, doing acid with strangers was consistent with my idea of a possible good time, so I shared a tab with them. When I started peaking, my hostess decided she had to go see her boyfriend, and there I was, alone with this guy, who, suddenly, was in my face.

He seemed to be coming on to me, but I wasn't sure. LSD is a potent drug, and on it, my perception was just short of hallucinatory. On top of that he was black and urban-poor, which meant that I, being very inexperienced and suburban-white, did not know how to read him the way I might have read another white kid from my own milieu. I tried to distract him with conversation, but it was hard, considering that I was having trouble with logical sentences, let alone repartee. During one long silence, I asked him what he was thinking. Avoiding my eyes, he answered, "That if I wasn't such a nice guy you could really be getting screwed." This sounded to me like a threat, albeit a low-key one. But instead of asking him to explain himself or leave, I changed the subject. Some moments later, when he put his hand on my leg, I let myself be drawn into sex because I could not face the idea that if I said no, things might get ugly. I don't think he had any idea of how unwilling I was—the cultural unfamiliarity cut both ways—and I suppose he may have thought that white girls just kind of lie there and don't do or say much. My bad time was made worse by his extreme gentleness; he was obviously trying very hard to turn me on, which, for reasons I didn't understand, broke my heart. Even as inexperienced as I was, I could see that he wanted a sweet time.

For some time after I described this event as "the time I was raped." I knew when I said it that the description wasn't accurate, that I had not said no, and that I had not been physically forced. Yet it *felt* accurate to me. In spite of my ambiguous, even empathic feelings for my unchosen partner, unwanted sex on acid is a nightmare, and I did feel violated by the experience. At times I even *elaborately* lied about what happened, grossly exaggerating the threatening words, adding violence—not out of shame or guilt, but because the pumped-up version was more congruent with my feelings of violation than the confusing facts. Every now and then, in the middle of telling an exaggerated version of the story, I would remember the actual man and internally pause, uncertain why I was saying these things or why they felt true—and then I would continue with the story. I am ashamed to admit this because it is embarrassing and because it conforms to the worst stereotypes of white women. I am also afraid the admission could be taken as evidence that women lie "to get revenge." My lies were told far from the event (I'd left Detroit), and not for revenge but in service of what I felt to be the metaphorical truth—although what that truth was is not at all clear to me, then or even now.

*

I remember my experience in Detroit, including the aftermath, every time I hear or read yet another discussion of what constitutes "date rape." I remember it when yet another critic castigates "victimism" and complains that everyone imagines himself or herself to be a victim and that no one accepts responsibility anymore. I could imagine telling my story as a verification that rape occurs by subtle threat as well as by overt force. I could also imagine casting myself as one of those crybabies who want to feel like victims. Both stories would be true and not true. The complete truth is more complicated than most of the intellectuals who have written scolding essays on victimism seem willing to accept. I didn't even begin to understand my own story fully until I described it to an older woman many years later, as proof of the unreliability of feelings. "Oh I think your feelings were reliable," she returned. "It sounds like you were raped. It sounds like you raped yourself." I didn't like her tone, but I immediately understood what she meant, that in failing to even try to speak up for myself, I had, in a sense, done violence to myself.

I don't say this in a tone of self-recrimination. I was in a difficult situation: I was very young and unready to deal with a such an intense culture clash of poverty and privilege, such contradictory levels of power and vulnerability, let alone ready to deal with it on drugs. But the difficult circumstances alone do not explain my inability to speak for myself. I was unable to effectively stand up for myself because I had never been taught how.

When I was growing up in the 60s, I was taught by the adult world that good girls did not have sex outside marriage and bad girls did. This rule had clarity going for it but little else; as it was presented to me, it allowed no room for what I actually might feel, what I might want or not want. Within the confines of this rule, I didn't count for much, and so I rejected it. Then came the less clear "rules" of cultural trend and peer example, which said that if you were cool you wanted to have sex as much as possible with as many people as possible. This message was never stated as a rule, but, considering how absolutely it was woven into the social etiquette of the day (at least in the circles I care about), it may as well have been. It suited me better than the adults' rule— it allowed me my sexuality at least—but again it didn't take into account what I might actually want or not want.

The encounter in Detroit, however, had nothing to do with being good or bad, cool or uncool. It was about someone wanting something I didn't want. Since I had only learned how to follow rules or social codes that were somehow more important than I was, I didn't know what to do in a situation where no rules obtained and that required me to speak up on my own behalf. I had never been taught that my behalf mattered. And so I felt helpless, even victimized, without really knowing why.

My parents and my teachers believed that social rules existed to protect me and that adhering to these rules constituted social responsibility. Ironically, my parents did exactly what many commentators recommend as a remedy for victimism. They told me that they loved me and that I mattered a lot, but this was not the message I got from the way they conducted themselves in relation to authority and social convention—which was not only that I didn't matter, but that *they* didn't matter. In this, they were typical of other adults I knew as well as of the culture around them. When I began to have trouble in school, both socially and academically, a counselor exhorted me to "just play the game"—meaning to go along with everything from social policy to the adolescent pecking order—regardless of what I thought of "the game." My aunt, with whom I lived for a short while, actually burned my jeans and T-shirts because they violated what she understood to be the standards of decorum. A close friend of mine lived in a state of war with her father because of her hippie clothes and hair—which were of course de rigueur among her peers. Upon discovering that she had been smoking pot, he had her institutionalized.

Many middle-class people—both men and women—have learned to equate responsibility with obeying external rules. And when the rules no longer quite apply, they don't know what to do—much like the enraged, gun-wielding protagonist of the movie *Falling Down*, played by Michael Douglas, who ends his ridiculous trajectory by helplessly declaring, "I did everything they told me to." If I had been brought up to reach my own conclusions about which rules were congruent with my particular experience of the world, those rules would've had more meaning for me. Instead, I was usually given a set of static pronouncements. For example, when I was thirteen, I was told by my mother that I couldn't wear a short skirt because "nice girls don't wear short skirts above the knee." I countered, of course, by saying that my friend Patty wore skirts above the knee. "Patty is not a nice girl," returned my mother. But Patty *was* nice. My mother is a very intelligent and sensitive person, but it didn't occur to her to define for me what she meant by "nice" and what "nice" had to do with skirt length, and how the two definitions might relate to what I had observed to be nice or not nice—and then let me decide for myself. It's true that most thirteen-year-olds aren't interested in, or much capable of, philosophical discourse, but that doesn't mean that adults can't explain themselves more completely to children. Part of becoming responsible is learning how to make a choice about where you stand in respect to the social code and then hold yourself accountable for your choice. In contrast, many children who grew up in my milieu were given abstract absolutes that were placed before us as if our thoughts, feelings, and observations were irrelevant.

*

Recently, I heard a panel of feminists on talk radio advocating that laws be passed prohibiting men from touching or making sexual comments to women on the street. Listeners called in to express reactions both pro and con, but the one I remember was a caller who said, "I'm an Italian woman. And if a man touches me and I don't want it, I don't need a law. I'm gonna beat the hell out of him." The panelists were silent. Then one of them responded in an uncertain voice, "I guess I just never learned how to do that." I understood that the feminist might not want to get into a fistfight with a man likely to be a lot bigger than she, but if her self-respect was so easily shaken by an obscene comment made by some random guy on the street, I wondered, how did she expect to get through life? She was exactly the kind of woman whom the cultural critics Camille Paglia and Katie Roiphe have derided as a "rape-crisis feminist"—puritans, sissies, closet-Victorian ladies who want to legislate the ambiguity out of sex. It was very easy for me to feel self-righteous, and I muttered sarcastically to my radio as the panel yammered about self-esteem.

I was conflicted, however. If there had been a time in my own life when I couldn't stand up for myself, how could I expect other people to do it? It could be argued that the grown women on the panel should be more capable than a sixteen-year-old girl on acid. But such a notion pre-supposes that people develop at a predictable rate or react to circumstances by coming to universally agreed-upon conclusions. This is the crucial unspoken presumption at the center of the date-rape debate as well as of the larger discourse on victimism. It is a presumption that in a broad but potent way reminds me of a rule.

Feminists who postulate that boys must obtain a spelled-out "yes" before having sex are trying to establish rules, cut in stone, that will apply to any and every encounter and that every responsible person must obey. The new rule resembles the old good girl/bad girl rule not only because of its implicit suggestion that girls have to be protected, but also by its absolute nature, its iron-fisted denial of complexity and ambiguity. I bristle at such a rule and so do a lot of other people. But should we really be so puzzled and indignant that another rule has been presented? If people have been brought up believing that to be responsible is to obey rules, what are they going to do with a can of worms like "date rape" except try to make new rules that they see as more fair or useful than the old ones?

The "rape-crisis feminists" are not the only absolutists here; their critics play the same game. Camille Paglia, author of *Sexual Personae*, has stated repeatedly that any girl who goes alone into a frat house and drinks is cruising for a gang bang, and if she doesn't know that, well, then she's an "idiot." The remark is striking not only for its crude unkindness but for its reductive solipsism. It assumes that all college girls have had the same life experiences as Paglia, and have come to the same conclusions about them. By the time I got to college, I'd been living away from home for years and had been around the block several times. I never went to a frat house, but I got involved with men who lived in rowdy boy-caves reeking of sex and rock and roll. I would go over, drink, and spend the night with my lover; it never occurred to me that I was in danger of being gang-raped, and if I had been, I would have been shocked and hurt. My experience, though some of it had been bad, hadn't led me to conclude that boys plus alcohol equals gang-bang, and I was not naïve or idiotic. Katie Roiphe, author of *The Morning After: Fear, Sex and Feminism on Campus*, criticizes girls who, in her view, create a myth of false innocence: "But did these twentieth-century girls, raised on Madonna videos and the six o'clock news, really trust that people were good until they themselves were raped? Maybe. Were these girls, raised on horror movies and glossy Hollywood sex scenes, really as innocent as all that?" I am sympathetic to Roiphe's annoyance, but I'm surprised that a smart chick like her apparently doesn't know that people process information and imagery with a complex subjectivity that doesn't in any predictable way alter their ideas about what they can expect from life. I trusted that the particular guys in their particular houses wouldn't rape me not because I was innocent, but because I was experienced enough to read them correctly.

Roiphe and Paglia are not exactly invoking rules, but their comments seem to derive from a belief that everyone except idiots interprets information and experience in the same way. In that sense, they are not so different from those ladies dedicated to establishing feminist-based rules and regulations for sex. Such rules, like the old rules, assume a certain psychological uniformity of experience, a right way.

The accusatory and sometimes painfully emotional rhetoric conceals an attempt not only to make new rules but also to codify experience. The "rape-crisis feminists" obviously speak for many women and girls who have been raped or *felt* raped in a wide variety of circumstances. They would not get so much play if they were not addressing a widespread and real experience of violation and hurt. By asking "Were they really so innocent?" Roiphe doubts the veracity of the experience she presumes to address because it doesn't square with hers or with that of her friends. Having not felt violated herself—even though she says she has had an experience that many would now call date rape—she cannot understand, or even quite believe, that anyone else would feel violated in similar circumstances. She therefore believes all the fuss to be a political ploy or, worse, a retrograde desire to return to crippling ideals of helpless femininity. In turn, Roiphe's detractors, who have not had her more sanguine "morning after" experience, believe her to be ignorant and callous, or a secret rape victim in deep denial. Both camps, believing their own experience to be the truth, seem unable to acknowledge the truth on the other side.

It is at this point that the "date-rape debate" resembles the bigger debate about how and why Americans seem so eager to identify themselves and be identified by others as victims. Book after article has appeared, written in baffled yet hectoring language, deriding the P.C. goody-goodies who want to play victim and the spoiled, self-centered fools who attend twelve-step programs, meditate on their inner child, and study pious self-help books. The revisionist critics have all had a lot of fun with the recovery movement, getting into high dudgeon those materially well-off people who describe their childhoods as "holocausts" and winding up with fierce exhortations to return to rationality before it's too late. Rarely do these critics make any but the most superficial attempt to understand why the population might behave thus.

In a fussing, fuming essay in these pages ("Victims, All?" October 1991) that has become almost a prototype of the genre, David Rieff expressed his outrage and bewilderment that affluent people would feel hurt and disappointed by life. He angrily contrasted rich Americans obsessed with their inner children to Third World parents concerned with feeding their actual children. On the most obvious level, the contrast is one that needs to be made, but I question Rieff's idea that suffering is one definable thing, that he knows what it is, and that since certain kinds of emotional pain don't fit this definition they can't really exist. This idea doesn't allow him to have respect for other people's experience—or even to see it. It may be ridiculous and perversely self-aggrandizing for most people to describe their childhood as a "holocaust," but I suspect that when people talk like that they are saying that as children they were not given enough of what they would later need in order to know who they are or to live truly responsible lives. Thus they find themselves in a state of bewildering loss that they can't articulate, except by wild exaggeration—much like I defined my inexplicable feelings after my Detroit episode. "Holocaust" may be a grossly inappropriate exaggeration. But to speak in exaggerated metaphors about psychic injury is not so much the act of a crybaby as it is a distorted desire to make one's experience have consequence in the eyes of others, and that such desperation comes from a crushing doubt that one's own experience counts at all *or is even real.*

In her book *I'm Dysfunctional, You're Dysfunctional,* Wendy Kaminer speaks harshly of women in some twelve-step programs who talk about being metaphorically raped. "It is an article of faith here that suffering is relative; no one says she'd rather be raped metaphorically than in fact," she writes, as if not even a crazy person would prefer a literal rape to a metaphorical one. But actually, I might. About a year after my "rape" in Detroit, I was raped for real. The experience was terrifying: my attacker repeatedly said he was going to kill me, and I thought he might. The terror was acute, but after it was over, it actually affected me less than many other mundane instances of emotional brutality I've suffered or seen other people suffer. Frankly, I've been scarred more by experiences I had on the playground in elementary school. I realize that may sound bizarre, but for me the rape was a clearly defined act, perpetrated on me by a crazy asshole whom I didn't know or trust; it had nothing to do with me or who I was, and so, when it was over, it was relatively easy to dismiss. Emotional cruelty is more complicated. Its motives are often impossible to understand, and it is sometimes committed by people who say they like or even love you. Nearly always it's hard to know whether you played a role in what happened, and, if so, what the role was. The experience *sticks* to you. By the time I was raped I had seen enough emotional cruelty to feel that the rape, although bad, was not so terrible that I couldn't heal quickly.

Again, my response may seem strange, but my point is that pain can be an experience that defies codification. If thousands of Americans say that they are in psychic pain, I would not be so quick to write them off as self-indulgent fools. A metaphor like "the inner child" may be silly and schematic, but it has a fluid subjectivity, especially when projected out into the world by such a populist notion as "recovery." Ubiquitous recovery-movement phrases like "We're all victims" and "We're all co-dependent" may not seem to leave room for interpretation, but they are actually so vague that they beg for interpretation and projection. Such phrases may be fair game for ridicule, but it is shallow to judge them on their face value, as if they hold the same meaning for everyone. What is meant by an "inner child" depends on the person speaking, and not everyone will see it as a metaphor for helplessness. I suspect that most inner-child enthusiasts use the image of themselves as children not so that they can *avoid* being responsible but to learn responsibility by going back to the point in time when they should have been taught responsibility—the ability to think, choose, and stand up for themselves—and were not. As I understand it, the point of identifying an "inner child" is to locate the part of of yourself that didn't develop into adulthood and then to develop it yourself. Whether or not this works is pretty questionable, but it is an attempt to accept responsibility, not to flee it.

*

When I was in my late teens and early twenties, I could not bear to watch movies or read books that I considered demeaning to women in any way; I reflexively evaluated what I saw or read in terms of the attitude it expressed towards women—or the attitude I *thought* it expressed. I was a very P.C. feminist before the term existed, and by the measure of my current understanding, my critical rigidity followed from my inability to be responsible for my own feelings. In this context, being responsible would have meant that I let myself feel whatever discomfort, indignation, or disgust I experienced without allowing those feelings to determine my entire reaction to a given piece of work. In other words, it would have meant dealing with my feelings and what had caused them, rather than expecting the outside world to assuage them. I could have chosen not to see the world through the lens of my personal unhappiness and yet maintained a kind of respect for my unhappiness. For example, I could have decided to avoid certain films or books because of my feelings without blaming the film or book for making me feel the way I did.

My emotional irresponsibility did not spring from a need to feel victimized, although it may have looked that way to somebody else. I essentially was doing what I had seen most mainstream cultural critics do; it was from them that I learned to view works of art in terms of the message they imparted and, further, that the message could be judged on the basis of consensual ideas about what life is, and how it can and should be seen. My ideas, like most P.C. ideas, were only slightly different from mainstream thought—they just shifted the parameters of acceptability a bit.

Things haven't changed that much: at least half the book and film reviews that I read praise or condemn a work on the basis of the likeability of the characters (as if there is a standard idea of what is likeable) or because the author's point of view is or is not "life-affirming"—or whatever the critic believes the correct attitude toward life to be. The lengthy and rather hysterical debate about the film *Thelma and Louise,* in which two ordinary women become outlaws after one of them shoots the other's would-be rapist, was predicated on the idea that stories are supposed to function as instruction manuals, and that whether the film was good or bad depended on whether the instructions were right. Such criticism assumes that viewers or readers need to see a certain type of moral universe reflected back at them or, empty vessels that they are, they might get confused or depressed or something. A respected mainstream essayist writing for *Time* faulted my novel *Two Girls, Fat and Thin* for its nasty male characters, which he took to be a moral statement about males generally. He ended his piece with the fervent wish that fiction not "diminish" men or women but rather seek to "raise our vision of" both—in other words, that it should present the "right" way to the reader, who is apparently not responsible enough to figure it out alone.

I have changed a lot from the P.C. teenager who walked out of movies that portrayed women in a demeaning light. As I've grown older, I've become more confident of myself and my ability to determine what happens to me and those images no longer have such a strong emotional charge; they don't *threaten* me in the same way. It's not that I think I'm safe, that I can't be hurt by misogyny in its many forms. I have been and can be. But I'm not so afraid of it that artistic representations of it viscerally disturb me, especially not if they are truthful depictions of how the artist sees his or her world, including the ugly elements. Stories or imagery like that help me to understand, to feel the ugly places in myself, to see the anguish and violence of it from somebody else's view, even if the view is a privileged one. The truth may hurt, but in art, anyway, it also helps, sometimes profoundly.

I consider my current view more balanced, but that doesn't mean my earlier feelings were wrong. The reason I couldn't watch "disrespect to women" at that time was that such depictions were too close to my own worst experience, and I found them painful. I was displaying a simplistic self-respect by not subjecting myself to something I was not ready to face. Being unable to separate my personal experience from what I saw on the screen, I was not dealing with my own personal experience—I think, paradoxically, because I hadn't yet learned to value it. It's hard to be responsible for something that isn't valuable. Someone criticizing me as dogmatic and narrow-minded would have had a point, but the point would've ignored the truth of my unacknowledged experience, and thus ignored me.

Many critics of the self-help culture argue against treating emotional or metaphoric reality as if it were equivalent to objective reality. I agree that they are not the same. But emotional truth is often bound up with truth of a more objective kind and must be taken into account. This is especially true of conundrums such as date rape and victimism, both of which are often discussed in terms of unspoken assumptions about emotional truth anyway. Sarah Crichton, in a cover story for *Newsweek* on "Sexual Correctness," described the "strange detour" taken by some feminists and suggested that "we're not creating a society of Angry Young Women. These are Scared Little Girls." The comment is both contemptuous and superficial; it shows no interest in *why* girls might be scared. By such logic, anger implicitly is deemed to be the more desirable emotional state because it appears more potent, and "scared" is used as a pejorative. It's possible to shame a person into hiding his or her fear, but if you don't address the cause of the fear, it won't go away. Crichton ends her piece by saying, "Those who are growing up in environments where they don't have to figure out what the rules should be, but need only follow what's been prescribed, are being robbed of the most important lesson there is to learn. And that's how to live." I couldn't agree more. But unless you've been taught how to think for yourself, you'll have a hard time figuring out your own rules, and you'll feel scared—especially when there is real danger of sexual assault.

After my experience in Detroit I was a lot more careful about getting high or drunk with people I didn't know. I never had another experience I could call "date rape" again. But sometimes I did find myself having sex with people I barely knew when I didn't really want to all that much. Sometimes I did it for the same reason I did in Detroit; I was secretly afraid things might get ugly if I said "no." But sometimes it was for a different reason that may be subtly related to the prior one: part of me wanted the adventure and that more questing side ran rough-shod over the side of me that was far more sensitive and shy. I'll bet the same thing happened to many of the boys with whom I had these experiences. Regardless of gender, all people have their strong, questing aspects as well as their more delicate aspects. If you haven't developed these characteristics in ways that are respectful of yourself and others, you will find it hard to be responsible for *any* of them. I don't think it's possible to develop yourself in such ways if you are attuned to following rules and codes that don't give your subjective experience enough importance.

I am not idealistic enough to hope that we will ever live in a world without rape and other forms of sexual cruelty; I think men and women will always have to make an effort to behave responsibly. But I think we could make the effort less difficult by changing the way we teach responsibility and social conduct. To teach a boy that rape is "bad" is not as effective as making him see that rape is a violation of his own masculine dignity as well as a violation of the raped woman. It's true that children don't know big words and that teenage boys may not be much interested in dignity. But these are things that children learn more easily by example, and learning by example runs deep.

*

When I was in my mid-thirties I invited to dinner at my home a man I'd known as a casual friend for two years. We'd had dinner and drinks a few times when I'd been on the East Coast; I was living on the West Coast where he was visiting, so he'd looked me up. In the original version of this essay, I wrote that I "didn't have any intention of becoming sexual with him," but it's closer to the truth to say that I didn't have strong intentions one way or the other. He was ten years younger than me and I wrongly assumed he wouldn't be interested in a woman my age—so I wasn't thinking about him that way either. But after dinner we slowly got drunk and soon were making out on the couch. I was ambivalent not only because I was drunk but because I realized that although part of me was up for it, the rest of me was not. So I began to say no. He parried each "no" with charming banter and became more aggressive. I went along with it for a time because I was charmed and touched by the sweet junior-high spirit of the thing. But at some point I began to be alarmed, and then he did and said some things that scared me. I don't remember the exact sequence of words or actions, but I do remember taking one of his hands in both of mine, looking him in the eyes and saying "If this comes to a fight you would win, but it would be very ugly for both of us. Is that really what you want?"

His expression changed and he dropped his eyes; shortly afterward he left.

In the original version of this essay I didn't mention that when I woke up the next day I couldn't stop thinking about him, and that when he called me I invited him over for dinner again. I didn't mention that we became lovers for the next two years. I just went on to say that I considered my decision to have been a responsible one "because it was made by taking both my vulnerable feelings and my carnal impulses into account," and that I "respected my friend as well by addressing both sides of his nature." I stand by what I originally wrote. But in omitting the aftermath of that "responsible decision" I was making the messy situation far too clear-cut, actually undermining my own argument by making it about propriety rather than the kind of fluid emotional negotiation that I see as necessary for personal responsibility.

In the original version of this essay, the last lines I wrote were: "It is not hard for me to make such decisions now, but it took me a long time to get to this point. I only regret that it took so long, both for my young self and for the boys I was with, under circumstances that I now consider disrespectful to all concerned."

But I don't truly regret most of the experiences I've had, even the half-hearted ones. They are part of who I am. The only circumstance I truly regret is the one I remember most vividly; the one in Detroit. Because as I remember him, that young "urban-poor" black man was no rapist. He was high on acid and misunderstanding, just as I was. If I had held his hands and looked in his eyes and said some version of "It could be ugly for both of us. Is that really what you want?" everything might've been different. I'm not sure. But I regret that I wasn't even able to try, and that I lied about it instead. Far more than any sex act, these lies were "disrespectful to all concerned."

The Bridge: A Memoir of St. Petersburg

In St. Petersburg Russia I got hit in the head with a bridge. It was a stone bridge, with a high arch and a low foot and a girdle of steel spotted with moss and green mold. There was a man walking across it with anger closing his face like a fist and a proud girl in a flashing skirt and a prancing dog looking up at them with eyes of love. We had just passed another boat full of screaming people, one of them a drunken man standing on the prow and acting like he was masturbating. I didn't see what he was doing at first so smiled at him: my husband laughed and said, "A guy goes by jerking off and you smile!"

We were in Russia teaching at a two-week writing conference. It didn't pay anything, but still we'd wanted to go: My husband's father had been born in Russia; he had escaped just before the Revolution, hidden under the straw of a vegetable cart with a bag of jewelry down his shirt and an earwig in his ear. He came to New York and ran a catering service. When he and his wife (a Finn) fought, they did it in Russian, and in this way Peter had learned a bit of the language. I had grown up seeing the Russian Premiere pounding a shoe on a table as he threatened to storm our houses and lawns. I found him terrible and wonderful, and when I was ten my parents gave me a subscription to a magazine called *Soviet Life* so that I could find out more about his country. Other girls played with Barbies and Beatle dolls with giant heads; they walked around with transistor radios held to their ears. I held *Soviet Life*, taking it out in school and covertly smoothing it open inside my desk to look at pictures of ballerinas with huge Soviet faces in pink feathered headdresses. I said I was going to be a writer, and that I would go to Russia and spy on it. Forty years later, I was a writer in a boat on the Neva with my writer husband. The day before Paul McCartney had played at the Hermitage; we could hear him and his band from our hotel blocks away, a dark roar of sound rolling through the streets, rolling past and present together.

If someone had told me when I was ten that I would grow up to be a writer, that I would be invited to read in Russia, and that a Beatle would be playing just a few blocks away, it would have made my life worth living. Now that it had all happened, I was simply put out by the lack of toilet seats and paper, the *giardia* in the water supply, and the animals starving in the streets because people put their pets out when they couldn't afford to feed them anymore.

During our six-hour layover at the Charles De Gaulle airport I had spent an hour running from toilette to toilette looking for a sink that had hot water so that I could wash my face. I burst from the last one with wild eyes complaining, "I never thought I'd say it, but maybe America really is better than every place else. Maybe our maniac government is right about maintaining our 'way of life,' and it really is our duty to take over everywhere and install hot water and toilets with seats. It's horrible about Iraq. But maybe it's finally worth it. My God, listen to me. I hate myself. But maybe it's the truth. Maybe it is!"

"Stop being a jackass," said Peter, but in a tolerant tone; we had been up all night and missed our connection. "A civilization is about more than plumbing."

"Yeah, it's also about buildings that stay up."

Soldiers with machines guns strolled past like animals with heavy paws. They gazed about as if longing to kill someone—anyone. Just weeks earlier a section of the airport had collapsed, and people *had* been killed.

"When I was in one of the stalls on the pot the attendant banged on the door and yelled at me. She poked her broom under the door to roust me out and I had just sat down!"

We laughed and went to a fancy bar and drank glasses of wine. Over the rim of my glass a group of aged, ragged people appeared as if a bag had been opened and they had come out of it. The two women had dust smeared on the backs of their skirts; one of them wore a brooch with its stone missing. The short man looked like a squashed head on a sack of clothes. The tall one had magnanimous eyes, a sclerotic nose and a liver-spotted white head. Even from a distance they exuded alcohol and urine; still, you could easily imagine the tall one twirling a walking stick. The maitre'd hesitated, then showed them to a table.

"Where do you suppose they're traveling to?" I asked.

"Maybe they're poor people who live in the airport. Though it's hard to believe they're French."

"It's hard to believe that attendant poked her broom under the door while I was having a moment of animal relief. I just hope the airport doesn't collapse on us. I hope terrorism doesn't get us."

*

The first bridge was so low even those of us sitting down had to put our heads in their laps; we shouted as we ducked, looked up to touch the molding steel roof of the stone mouth, then looked back down at its lapping black liquid tongue. I shouted with these people like I talked with them—excitedly, eagerly. All day and night we talked, in cafeterias, conference rooms and bars, about

Islamic extremism in Indonesia, American atrocities in Iraq, AIDS in Russia, our families, phobias and times we had lost our bags. Earlier that day I had talked to a writer from Kenya, a big man with deep, reasonable eyes and a richly glistening head. He had just lead a panel discussion on African literature and was taking a cigarette break in a damp hallway painted a dull salmon. He rolled a cigarette as we talked about what was shocking to African readers, which was mostly homosexuality and black women having sex with white men. Recently, he said, an African woman had written from a white man's perspective about his lust for a fat black woman, and it had been accepted quite warmly. We talked about the ways in which the unacceptable could be not merely accepted but adored; he gave as an example his Kenyon neighbor who went around in jeweled robes and a turban and blasted the neighborhood with every recording Maria Callas ever made; in spite of the boys seen leaving his back porch early in the morning, people did not revile him as a queer, but instead revered him as a lovable eccentric. When a neighbor's son called him "homo" the gentleman demanded a public apology and got it when the father frog-marched the kid over in full view of everyone. In response I told him about Sweet Evenin' Breeze, a black hermaphrodite hospital orderly much beloved in my parent's southern town, even by racists—the writer from Kenya paused in rolling his cigarette, a hot expression coming up through his layers of eye. He held it back and continued rolling his cigarette, and I continued talking about my grandfather who, when my 8-year-old mother asked "Why is that man wearing a dress?" answered, "Honey, that's not a man, that's an accident of nature. That's Sweet Evenin' Breeze."

"So strange," mused the Kenyan writer. "In some place inside them, people accept it all, as long as you keep to the conventions." In the courtyard outside two dogs tore up an old hunk of bread. In my head my mother kept talking. "And he walked on down the street in this funny way," she said. "Like a woman, you know."

*

The screaming became a shapeless roar. *Like a woman, you know.* The previous night there had been fighting in the hotel; we heard shouting and somebody's fist beating a door. They were fighting over a woman.

*

My parents had argued once about Sweet Evenin' Breeze. People were over visiting, and my mother was describing to them how the whole racist town had loved the hermaphrodite orderly.

"Our town was not all racist," said my father, "don't slander us."

"Sam Blackburn was a real racist and you know it," she said.

"Sam Blackburn was not a racist!" He almost shouted it. "When Sam was in for a hernia, Sweets was the only one he would let hold him. He said, 'Only Sweets knows how to hold me without it hurting.'"

*

We came out the open mouth; everybody sat up and cheered. On the stone bank two boys walked on their hands, one after the other. There were more cheers; one of the boys held his legs erect, the other let them dangle at the knee. Overhead, clouds parted and freed bursts of lavender rimmed with orange.

"Are you still sorry we came?" asked my husband.

"I don't know," I said, dazed. Another boat of drunken people plowed past, roaring lustily. "It's strange to be floating through, seeing all these things and not being able to understand or to fully experience them. But it's beautiful here and powerful in a way America isn't."

We ducked under another bridge. Its shadow woke at our passing and tossed like an ogre with the boat lights prickling its skin.

*

Days before, I had given a reading with an American writer named Jeff who'd read about an escaping slave hiding his son in the ass of a white cow, then finding him later shit out and his skin mysteriously covered in a layer of white. We'd gone to dinner with him and his fiancée Danielle and our Russian host Mischka; Danielle was a sexy, thick-bodied beauty with fake mauve nails and a skeptical attitude towards all writing, including her fiancé's. She ordered absinthe and tiger shrimp and then out of nowhere snapped at Jeff, "What's wrong, too ghetto for you?" He looked hurt but forbearing.

From a bright, heat-steaming kitchen window, blue eyes stared out, suspicious and crouched in their expression. Mischka was saying, "Young people feel that when we were Soviet at least we were number one. Everyone hated us but it was okay because also they were afraid of us. We were number one." American rock music played on the sound system, but I was thinking of ballerinas in pink Soviet headdresses. In the world we were at war with Iraq, but when I dreamed of it, it was Russian soldiers who fought us. In the dream, Arabic women in veils saved me when the Russian soldiers came.

*

Another tunnel roared over us; we sailed out past a huge pale-green building with beautiful beetling brows. It glanced at us, sighed and folded its hands across its mid-section as it returned its attention to the past. In the recent past, we had visited the

Museum of the Defense and Siege of Leningrad. It was a small apartment up a short flight of stairs lined with great crude paintings of Stalin and the generals he had murdered in gilt frames. Deeper in were more paintings depicting dead half-eaten horses lying in the streets, gutted buildings and the city exploding under a flaming sky of clotted oil. Hung just beneath them were enlarged newspaper cartoons of Hitler driving a pack of goggle-eyed Nazi dogs, military maps and Soviet uniforms stiff and small enough for chloroformed children. On the floor were hoary broken-legged cannon, some shocked household items, tables of personal effects (buttons, ribbons, a diary with two pages filled in) and a broken loaf of sawdust bread ringing with starvation like a shell rings with the sea. A small dim diorama protected a table, a rug, a chair, a child's corn husk toy, and a wooden radio with a metronome sounding from the torn gold fabric of its speaker. "They played the sound of the metronome twenty-four hours a day," said Peter. "It meant that the heart of Leningrad still beat."

*

Clouds rolled in, white and profoundly blue, massed like great intense thoughts in a clear and joyfully humming mental field. A little blimp toiled distantly, finite, curved and occluded in the great mind of the sky. The Kenyon guy stood up to take a picture.

*

Two days before Peter and I had gone to the Hermitage, the giant palace full of gold furniture, carriages, priceless art and knick-knacks; in a pamphlet we read that after the Revolution a delegation of peasants staying in there got drunk and shat in the gold tureens, vases and marble baths. The next day, in the Siege of Leningrad Museum, we saw photographs of the peasants'

33

emaciated sons with their limbs blown off—both legs and an arm in the case of one son, a large-eyed young man who stared raptly at the left-hand corner of the frame, his up-turned face stunned as if by the glimpse of another world. "So moving," said Peter. The gray museum attendant coughed in the next room.

*

When I told Danielle about the peasants shitting in the tubs she made a disgusted face. She'd suddenly turned to a table full of students, picked up a stray manuscript and began reading it ferociously. She asked if she could sit in on my class. "I want to see if it's a game," she said.

"It is," I said, "to some extent."

*

The water flexed its cold rolling muscle; the boat was turning slow and hard. After the war the peasants' sons were starved again, shot and worked to death in prisons. Today their daughters sat in the streets and begged. Every day we passed them, old women holding out cups or caps or selling bunches of flowers. The previous night a group of us passed one of these old women on our way to dinner at an expensive restaurant that was cheap for us. One of the writers looked at her and spoke in English. "Did you shelter any Jews?" he asked. Hopefully, she extended her cup. "I don't think so," he said, walking past.

Later, the organizers amused us over dinner, describing the time a writer had gotten lost in the subway system and been held prisoner by some toughs who slapped him, robbed him and wouldn't let him go until he'd said "I am not the writer—you are the writers" fifty times, in Russian. "And they were probably right," said Peter, laughing.

Outside the window another old lady stood and shouted in at us. "What is she saying?" I asked Mischka. He listened for a moment and then said "I think she's asking how we make our money. She's asking, do we even work."

*

We sailed along on the Neva's lilting silver skin, listening to someone tell a story about the time one of Stalin's men put on a show for his boss by mimicking a purged apparatchik pleading shrilly for his life. Stalin roared with laughter, he gasped, "Stop, stop!" and pounded his knee.

"Did he kill the guy who told the story?" asked a student.

"Of course!"

The Kenyon author sat down and put away his camera.

I wish I had not thrust racists on him while he was rolling his cigarette. I could've told a different story. I could've told him that many years ago I had been a dancer, a stripper, in clubs and sometimes bars for guys who hated queers, who might beat and even kill them, and that on one evening I had watched a room of these guys become enchanted by a troop of queers lip-synching and dancing as women. But then he might not have accepted me.

*

We were coming to a fork in the river, one direction of which was marked by a portal made of stone walls. There was a window of broken brick in one of the walls, and the midnight sun came through it, giving the river a restless patina of mauve and peach. In the distance was another bridge, a low embankment of ocher stone that curved round a wooded bend; beyond that was a meadow, a glimpse of forest, an enchanted lake of red and fiery purple streaming through the sky. Someone yelled, "I want to go there!"

And music came from below. In the hold, a Russian boy was playing a tape so a Russian girl would dance with him. *This is a man's world*—It was a James Brown song nearly forty years old, and it joined past and present with its saturating voice. *But it wouldn't be nothing*—Brown's voice was so dramatic that it made even the spaces between sounds glow with density and mass. *Without a woman or a girl*—The Russian boy pulled the smiling girl stiffly towards him. In my memory, a strip club dancer leaned against a velvet pillar, his eyes down, one leg bent, one small knee tensely flexed, lithe white belly pressed moodily out as he arched his back, ecstatic and abject in the pale grainy light, and shining in the slow glandular fire of someone else's voice. *Man thinks about the little baby girl*—Jeff and Danielle gently touched their faces together. We came near the enchanted place. *And the baby boy*—Down below, the boy and girl bantered, she tanned and blond with sad, tired eyes and a long, sinewy neck; he white-skinned, with little burning blue eyes and a lewd red mouth. He was slight and effeminate, but there was something wild in him, leaping like a goblin in a dark and ancient forest. You would feel that with him inside you, his blue eyes promised you would feel it. But the girl just laughed; she'd already felt it in herself. *Man makes money*—Eyes down, the naked dancer twirled his raiment of grainy light. The audience of men sat at their tables, getting teary as they lifted their beers. *To buy from other men*—

"I want to go there!" But we couldn't; the song was over, and the portal was closed off with a rusted chain. There was a sigh of disappointment. I closed my eyes, tired. "My name is really Traci," said Danielle. "I changed it when I got old enough." She'd said this at the bar, over golden-mouthed drinks. The ballerinas in their feathered headdresses fluttered up through the murk. "He said only Sweets could hold me and not hurt me." But Sweet

Evenin' Breeze, with a lithe movement of his little hips, parted the darkness like it was a curtain, slipped inside it and disappeared.

*

"Walk the dog! Walk the dog!" Another bridge was coming, and boaters were shouting up at the people walking across it. Peter looked back at me and smiled; we put our heads down. A wing of foam took us forward. When I was ten I slept in a red brick house in a row of red brick houses on lawns of bright sod, and dreamed of spying on Russia and writing books. Girls pressed their transistor radios to their ears and played with Beatle dolls that had tiny bodies and huge flawless heads. I had finally come but Russia was broken; the lavender was pouring through and Paul McCartney was playing at the Hermitage, unintelligible but horribly audible blocks away. He had broken free of his tiny doll body but now he had no shape. "Walk the dog, walk the dog!" I raised my head. There was a girl with a flashing skirt and a prancing dog. "Walk the dog!" I raised my head again; there was a man leaning over the rail, his face a fist of longing and rage. I thought, *Everything is too mixed now, too many things are mixed. I am too small to hold it all, and if I try I will break.*

And then I was hit, as if by a blunt knife wielded like a punch. "What is it?" cried Peter and we went under the bridge. Down under, I thought, where giant flowers lift and fall with the deepest waves. "Mary," he said, "are you alright?"

"I don't know. I feel sick." One of the flowers was a girl's face; she was rising to meet me, one eye alive, the other not. Her name was Valeria and the memory of her came with terrible feeling.

"God, look at the blood!"

We had come out the other side of the bridge; there was blood on my head. I had not thought of that girl in years. "Peter," I said. "I'm afraid."

Mischka came towards us; he looked like he was thinking, *Oh no*. My vision began to blur. "I just remembered this girl," I said to Peter. "Somebody hit her and she fell asleep and when she woke up she wasn't right." One part of his eye came towards me; everything else in him moved away. I saw it all before me: a dark city street with its torn paper and discarded cans, a bag of spilled cashews, a wheel or flashing neon color. Then my vision blurred so I could barely see at all.

"We're right here sweetheart," said Peter.

"Don't let me fall asleep," I said, then fell.

*

It was dark were I fell; there were no giant flowers. But there were voices, hundreds of voices, unintelligible but still glimmering and filling the dark with movement. The dark had several strands of movement, each one a narrow door, all spinning so fast I did not see how I could choose the right one. But I did not have to choose; it chose me. It drew me in like I was smoke, and I was gone.

Imagine a bird flying in the dark of night. Suddenly, it flies into the rafters of a house; down below it there is a party with people eating and drinking. Adults are talking and dancing lustily, kids are laughing and running between them. All of life is there with its lights, sounds, smells. Life rises up and pierces the bird's supple breast; the bird flies out the other end of the rafters and into the night again. It sees and knows and instantly forgets everything but the rhythmic beating of its own wings.

At first I was a bird. I saw, knew and forgot everything. Then I was a person who knew nothing. I was at the party. People were drinking and eating; the room roared with their talking and laughing. Who were they? Music was playing. But something was wrong. I was curled in a corner naked. Something bad had happened, what was it? Should I cover my nakedness or show it? A bird flew overhead and disappeared. A sharp smell flew up my nose; there was the blue-eyed Russian boy with smelling salts. As he drew away he looked at me intensely and I saw the sexy goblin in his eyes. His eyes flashed pleasure at my seeing. I fell back again, though not so deep this time.

This time I was not naked at a party. I was curled safe in my bed. On one side of me was a wheel of color and spilled cashews. On the other was Peter's hand. "I'm right here," he said. I could feel his warmth and fear but I could not see him. "They're stopping the boat," he said. "We're going to the hospital." I couldn't see. I was blind. This was the bad thing. This was my nakedness.

"How you doin'?" said Danielle. She was in front of me; I could feel her warmth and curiosity.

"I can't see," I said.

"You'll be fine," said Danielle. "Trust me."

"But I can't see."

"Oh God," said Peter.

"Yes you *can* see." I felt her hands on mine. Warm, with plastic nails and rings. "You're looking right at me."

"But that's what I mean. I can't see you."

Instead I saw the girl who got hit and went to sleep. I could see Valeria, obese and swollen, with dulled eyes and a slack mouth, moving absently on a dirty stage, half-aware of the men sitting rows before her. Maybe half-aware too of my pity and terror coming towards her from someplace far away.

"You *can* see, you *can* see."

"Traci," I said, "I'm afraid. I'm really afraid."

"You're going to be fine. I've seen worse, believe me."

"But I—"

And then I saw Traci/Danielle. I saw her lips and teeth first, flashing slightly, as if in a darkened room. I saw Valeria too. From a distance the dull eyes and mouth, even the obese white flesh seemed to know something not sayable in words. Something I was about to know for the rest of my life and be unable to say. It would be terrible but I must accept it because Valeria had.

Danielle came fully before me, glossy-haired, radiant and snappy, the gold of her jewelry cast on her skin. I saw from her expression that she had not been trying to help me as much as boss me. But she had helped anyway and I was grateful for it.

"We're here," said Peter, and he took my arm.

I broke away to kiss Danielle's forehead. "You're a wonderful person," I said. "Thank you." And for the first time I felt fear come from her, mixed with confusion and surprise.

We crossed over to land on a little wooden plank. A car had stopped and the blond Russian girl was leaning into it, persuading the drunk kid at the wheel to drive us to the hospital for some rubles. He agreed. Two rumpled girls climbed out of the front seat, smoothing their hair. "He says please excuse the mess," said the blond girl, and we climbed over a mound of refuse into the panting car. The kid looked curiously at me and hit the gas with one arm out the window.

Because I was with the writer's conference I went to The American Clinic, where they spoke English, gave you a private room and a toilet with a seat. The doctor had a high, reserved chest, a gentle, slightly bitter mouth and precise eyes that held their object like gleaming tweezers. He was not interested in my brain, but it was his duty to take care of it and so he would.

My husband sat on the bed with me while we waited for the X-rays, and I told him about the girl who had come up to meet me on my way down.

"Several strippers I worked with were beautiful, but she was the most beautiful. Black hair, full lips, long legs, big breasts—she looked like Vampirella, except on stage, there was nothing fierce about her. She didn't dance, she posed in an almost trance-like way. Though she did have a powerful look in her eyes sometimes, and her eyes were deep. She did this complicated 'stocking act,' where she would hook the stocking on the end of her toe and change position, stretching it this way and that, so that she was looking at it over her shoulder, etc. She'd make it this precise, balletic thing, like a narcissistic ritual, her alone in her room— and then she'd look up and give the men these hot, deep eyes, and let them in the room with her. Let them inside *her*, but for just a second, then she was back with the stockings. That was the strip tease really, this placid beauty who suddenly showed herself. Or seemed to. It's the cheapest trick, but she didn't realize that, which is why it worked.

"The place was an old-fashioned strip joint—the men didn't have any contact with the girls, there was no sticking money in underwear, no tipping allowed, though of course girls would accept it if it was a big enough bill. Men would sometimes scream obscene abuse, but they also wrote love letters, with cash or little presents, hoping the girl would meet them. One of them, a journalist, fell in love with Valeria, and did a big story on her in the city magazine.

"The magazine did her hair and make-up like she was a 40s movie star, and they put her on the cover with a tiara on her head. The journalist described going to see her night after night, fantasizing that she was *une belle dame sans merci*. Then, when he got to meet her for the article, he found out she was just an ordinary 22-year-old from a small town in northern Quebec, the kind of kid who ordered a Blue Zombie just to see what it was."

The journalist had described that moment so vividly I could recall it clearly almost thirty years later; at the private island of their table, the young man looks with abashed disappointment at the impossible girl reaching for a frosted blue drink loaded with umbrellas and striped straws. There is the waiter's retreating arm, the jaundiced light from the bar glowing about the dark heads of strangers.

Valeria started coming to work in low-cut white dresses with cinched waists and frothy skirts, and fancy broad-brimmed hats with flowers. When she came in, men would turn around and say "There she is!" Women sometimes would come back to the dressing room and ask for her autograph.

"What a great story," said Peter. "It would never happen today, and it's wonderful."

It was wonderful. Then one night a bunch of us left work at midnight and went out for drinks. It was summer, the street was crowded with sweating, half-dressed people, and the air was heavy, like something had burst inside it and swelled it with juice. Again and again hot rhythmic neon burst and dissolved against the night sky. Valeria wanted to get a bag of cashews, so we stopped at a stand. She was wearing a fancy dress and a big lacy hat, and a red-faced man scratching his scabby chest through his open shirt stopped dead and gawked. "Great God!" he screamed. "You are beautiful!" We all ignored him as he followed us down the street screaming "You're beautiful!" until finally he screamed "You're beautiful but you stink, you stinking whore!" She flew at him so fast her cashews sprayed the street; he shrank back, blinking and weaving his head confusedly. She screamed as loud as he did, "I don't stink, you stink man, too bad for me to talk to!" For a second a bolt of feeling connected them. Then he swung on her, hitting just hard enough to knock her off balance. She wobbled on her high heels, then fell and banged her head on the curb. The record store light flashed like an explosion. Somebody cursed him. He jerked his head fiercely, wiped his mouth and walked away on bowed, toiling legs. The cashew man ran to get a cup of water to revive Valeria, but by the time he got back she'd come to and was sitting on the curb brushing off her hat.

Later she sat in the bar, drinking Blue Zombies and bragging. "Some people would just take it," she said. "But not me. I'm proud, and I don't let nobody get away with saying that shit. I fight back."

The next day she didn't show up for work. Two days later one of the sound men broke into her apartment and found her asleep. She didn't wake up for a week; when she did her mouth was slack and her eyes unmoored.

We were quiet a long moment. Peter kissed my temple and said, "When you were out I had your forehead cupped in my hand the whole time." We were quiet some more.

The X-ray was okay. We each lay down in a crooked, creaking bed. Half-asleep Peter said, "I'm sorry about your friend." Light came under the door crack.

"She wasn't really my friend," I said. "That's why I forgot until now."

"Still," said Peter.

"I know."

The room stretched out and became enormous between our beds. Peter began to snore. I turned and scratched myself and felt my head with my fingers.

Fifteen years ago I had returned to the town where I had been a stripper with Valeria. I had come to participate in a literary festival. The little club where we used to dance still existed but had become seedy and charmless. There was no pretense of a show; women stomped across the stage, then stripped and squatted to let men finger-fuck them for tips. I asked the bouncer if anyone from the old days was still there; Valeria was the only name he knew. She had gotten fat, he said, and puffy from alcohol and drugs. He glanced at the stage to be sure the finger-fucking hadn't turned ugly, then looked back at me and tapped his forehead. "Other problems too," he said.

I turned and turned and tried to calm my breath. The wordless knowledge I had seen when I could not see was near me but not on me; for now I would be spared it. I tried to give it a form, a garment, a hem I could cling to, and lay my head against. But it had no form, no garment. Light grew and elongated under the vinyl blind, revealing a layer of dreaming dust. How gentle it was, the light and dust, the cheaply painted sill, the blind.

Peter stirred "Are you okay?" he said in a furred voice.

"Yes. I think so."

Outside a woman shouted a string of words, a grudging and slatternly command; she was answered by a torrent of hammers, a storm of industry and hopelessness. Peter got up and looked out the window. Construction was underway; violence echoed between the buildings in rising red rings of sound. "That's the most primitive scaffolding I've ever seen," he said. "There's nothing to keep them from falling off."

A technician, a middle-aged woman in a low-cut blouse and high heels, put my head in a long silver tube and took its picture with an ecstatic, spinning camera. She and Peter looked at the pictures, spoke Russian and laughed. "She says everything is working fine," he said. "But is not so cute! She said that!"

When we got back to our hotel we stopped by the conference office. People were lunching on canned meat, bread and cold blintzes, eating off a low coffee table and from plates on their knees. The blond girl from the boat was there; her knees, small and bruised-looking without any bruise, were nearly as expressive as her eyes. She got up to give me tea in a plastic cup; she touched my shoulder and told me that everyone was distracted and upset about the disappearance of a student, a flaky, blowsy girl who had last been seen getting very drunk with Russian guys.

"Things like this happen every year," said one of the organizers, a small, scrappy American named Jeff. "People come to St. Petersburg and enter a chaos vector. But it always works out. Anyway, I'm glad you're okay."

Peter came up and we sat down for some canned meat and bread. Mishka came in and embraced me. "I know what you went through," he said. "Me and my friends all had concussions. To get out of the Afghan war we bashed our heads on the wall of the military building—" he jerked his head to show me—"we vomit and black out and don't have to go."

Peter went down to the café to check his email, and I went down the hall to our room. The windows in our room were enormous and screen-less, and took up most of the wall. I stood up on the wide sill and looked out, into the smaller windows across the street. On their sills were clay pots, the bent stems and leaves of plants, small jars and bottles lined up neatly and the wily ears of a cat not yet put out. A mirror gleamed; a swollen hand methodically used a brush. The wind filled the air with white down. The curtains were a rough synthetic, a blend of pink and orange that put a glow on the room—lurid, artificial, but with a hint of the ideal. I shut them, and got into bed. The bent leaves, the ears, the little jars, the swollen hand, the drifting down; each came through the synthetic pores and was transformed into a garment whose wearer I could not see but trusted nonetheless. I lay my head on its hem and went dreamlessly to sleep.

*

In my class the next day a stray red kitten came in the door and walked the length of the conference table with its tail up. The missing student came back, laughed and said, "Couldn't you tell, those guys were gay!" We feasted on blintzes, herring and borscht. We went to the opera to see *Carmen* and sat next to Jeff and Danielle. The players were thin and seemed tired; Carmen's voice was tremulous and yearning, her shoulders were small and hunched, which she tried to hide by putting her hands on her unconfident hips. Danielle said Beyoncé was better in the MTV Hip Hop era version; Peter said "But this one has such a soft expressive throat." Jeff said we should've gone to see *The Nose* instead. We had cake and caviar during intermission, then came back to the penetrating scent of fresh piss wafting through our box from the lavatory's open door. The painted cherub on the wall next to us had a crumbling foot and I thought the whole box might crumble, and pitch us into the human sea below.

But the orchestra played jauntily, the dancers gamely twirled their skirts. Aged matadors with turtle eyes stumped across the stage with their old backs staunchly humped. When we came out, the streets were full of girls wearing tight shirts with plunging necklines and light-colored pants with dark thongs showing underneath, and deep-eyed boys fiercely escorting them. Rattling cars came at us in waves; a clock tower too, defaced by too much gold bore down, and a giant rearing horse.

I took Peter's hand. He raised his arm. A car stopped for us, not a taxi, just a young guy wanting to make extra money. Peter told him where we were going and negotiated a price. The driver's face, sideways in the side mirror, was beautiful and full of wasted strength. He turned the wheel and took us into a speeding gray curve of traffic, nearly colliding with an oppositional curve. Above us clouds continued to move, slow and round, and massively white at the top.

2004

Worshipping the Overcoat: An Election Diary

Day One

When I saw Sarah Palin speak at the Republican convention, the hair on the back of my neck stood up. I had thought McCain's choice of running mate must mean that he was in a complete paranoid tailspin, the kind that come before huge, humiliating defeats. But as I watched her, and the rabid, adoring response to her, I thought something else which was: this woman is a sadist and she doesn't know it. And it's working for her; her people love her for that very reason, and they don't know it.

By "sadist" I don't mean a costume-wearing fetishist, and if I did, I wouldn't be as appalled. I mean something more basic, a person whose driving motive in life is to dominate, control and inflict pain. Most people don't know what their driving motive is, and most people have more than one. But some people have one that is so unconflicted and so overwhelming that they fairly drip with it. What I was looking at on stage at the Republican Convention was somebody who dripped with highly charged, puerile cruelty; it was there in her sneering, aggressively charming voice, in her body, in the set of her mouth. It was there also in the roaring response to her, a response that comes from the body, while the head is thinking something else altogether, about loving America, standing up to terrorists, whatever.

When I said to people "I think Sarah Palin is a sadist," they reacted like I was making a joke, or being provocative. I suppose that I was. But how far off was I? What do you call it when she incites crowds to threaten Obama with death by calling him a terrorist, in that dripping, girlish voice? These are people who are looking to hurt someone, and their urge has just been legitimized, even idealized for them by an attractive woman whom some young men I know consider "hot."

Day Two

This election makes me remember Vladimir Nabokov's essay on Nikolai Gogol's "The Overcoat," in which he describes the short story as "a grotesque and grim nightmare making black holes in the dim pattern of life;" it is a beautiful, flexible and fantastically broad phrase. "The Overcoat" is about a poor half-crazy little clerk in pre-Revolutionary Russia who, when his thin coat rots off his back one freezing winter, spends his entire savings on having a new coat made for him. The new coat is magnificent, and it transforms his life. For the first time he is invited to a party where he drinks too much; on the way home he is robbed of his coat; the robbery breaks his heart; he sickens and dies. The story is typically read as an allegory of "the little guy" in a socially unjust world, but Nabokov sees something more terrible, a story of "whirling masks," through which the tortured human protagonist must wander in desperate confusion, and in which the true plot, as opposed to the literal one, comes from "that secret depth of the human soul where the shadows of other worlds pass like the shadows of nameless and soundless ships."

How garish are these masks that talk to us non-stop every day, how huge they loom out of television and cyberspace! What secret depths do they come from, what primitive forces are

48

finding expression through them? What the fuck are they doing here? John McCain, having unleashed insane Pandora, is now trying to stuff her back in the box probably because human beings are horrified at seeing his rallies turn into pre-lynch mobs. But when one of his supporters denounces Obama as "an Arab," and McCain responds like a person ("He's a decent family man"), he's booed by his own. While one of his masks makes nice, the others keep putting out the misinformation. Through it all wanders the human voter—who, if he's Republican, bought the overcoat years ago and, though it's been stolen from him, still worships it on his knees.

Day Three

The most visible story of John McCain has been his "honor" and how important it is to him, how key to the understanding of his mind. The less visible story is his violent temper: how he yells at people for nothing, nearly attacks people who frustrate him, how he once called his wife a "cunt" in front of reporters. Now the anger has come out in a hugely visible form, projected like a demon into the screaming herds that accuse Obama of terrorism as they run bellowing off a cliff.

A melancholy thought: McCain may once have had honor, or at least a concept of it. If he still has enough decency to be ashamed of losing it he needs anger to hide his shame; without his anger he would not be able to bear his shame.

Day Four

When Hillary Clinton and Barack Obama were still fighting for the nomination, I had a conversation with a woman who said she supported Hillary because "any female" would be preferable to "any male," and that she thought Obama was no different from anyone else in the male system. When Sarah Palin got nominated I asked her, did she support her? "Of course not," she said. "Sarah

Palin is not a woman, I don't care how many times she's given birth. She's totally bought into the male power system."

I thought, how ridiculous. Then my husband reminded me of Fritz Lang's *Metropolis* and the false Maria. In the movie, the real Maria is a working-class girl trying to help her fellows by pure-hearted means. The rulers then build a false Maria to sow division and hatred. It doesn't quite work as a comparison; Palin is more a combination of what the real Maria claims to be (evangelical) and what the false one is, proud and violent. But the film's logic is visual, and visually, it pictures America now as it once pictured Weimar Germany. The false Maria's dance is one of gluttony and power, and it has a demonic force that awakens ancient archetypes of chaos and destruction. And the damn thing even winks.

Check it out: www.youtube.com/watch?v=oFfa3Qa4ah4

Day Five
When Hillary was still running, I didn't support her because I preferred Obama, and because I didn't think she could win. Somebody asked me if I thought she couldn't win because she's a woman, and I said "Not because she's a woman, but because she's not enough of a cunt." I meant that she didn't have a raw female presence equal to that of her husband, Bill. I went on to say that as a liberal (sort of) woman, I didn't think she'd dare go there, that the only woman who could do that would be a conservative. I was right, and I have never been more sorry. Sarah Palin has the kind of glandular force I was referring to, something which has nothing to do with her prettiness, but augments it immeasurably. Hillary Clinton was taunted for being strong—privately, even liberals made her out as a castrator, which was brutally unfair: like many professional women, Hillary never cut off anyone's nuts but her own. No one's taunting Sarah Palin like that and no wonder: Hillary is accomplished verbally; her power comes from the part

of the body with teeth. Palin can't talk her way out of a bag; she doesn't need to. That's not the source of her power.

Day Six

The language aspect of the Obama/McCain debate was the usual rote push-pull. When I turned down the sound, the picture was clearer and more alarming. McCain was malign, contemptuous and very physical. Obama was weak, vague and heady. McCain looked like a big, vicious dog, Obama like a smaller dog trying to avoid a fight by looking away and licking his lips a lot. It was very dispiriting to see.

Day Seven

My sister has an eerie ability to look at people and "read" them very quickly in terms of their character; I have rarely known her to be wrong. She was the first person to tell me, years before the election, that Obama was great, that he needed to run for president. "He has white light glowing around his head," she said.

The second person to say anything to me about Obama is a writer friend. She said she liked him a lot, but that she worried about him as a leader because she couldn't "feel his dick." She wasn't talking about sex. She meant that he didn't fully, on a bodily level, believe in himself, that his actions came totally from his head. I agree with her. That is what makes him look fragile sometimes, especially in contrast with John McCain, whose dick, like it or not, one *can* feel. McCain's confidence is ghastly, because it is so caught up in his violent righteousness—but it is there.

In a strange way, these two qualities, the powerful, glowing mind and the lack of full bodily presence are part of what make Obama a compelling and emotional figure. Whatever he has accomplished, it has been through the power of his mind, that almost other-worldly glow that has carried him through so many obstacles, especially vicious race-prejudice. So many of us know what it is to lack confidence, yet to will yourself to go on, even though you don't quite feel the ground under your feet. People are calling McCain the "underdog" now, but this is bullshit. Obama, who's barely ahead in the polls, was always the underdog here—black people were scared to vote for him at first because they thought he'd be killed. And they had reason to fear. He has incredible courage to be where he is, up against that old bastard, especially if he got there without full confidence. My sister believes he can win. I hope she is right.

2008

Leave the Woman Alone!: On the Never-Ending Political Extra-Marital Scandals

When the Eliot Spitzer scandal* erupted a year and a half ago, I found myself more than usually irritated at the lavish sympathy directed at his wife, Silda Spitzer, who was presumed to be deeply humiliated by people who had no way of knowing what she was feeling; this sympathy was *so* lavish that at times it bore a striking resemblance to gloating. It was the way Hilary Clinton was talked about (though the gloating was more upfront in that case) and the way Elizabeth Edwards† would be talked about, at least until her book *Resilience* came out, when with quite remarkable speed that out-sized sympathy turned to out-sized contempt—suggesting to me that it had been contempt all along.

---

*On March 10, 2008, *The New York Times* reported that Governor of New York Eliot Spitzer had patronized a prostitution ring run by an escort service known as Emperors Club VIP. During the course of an investigation into Emperors Club VIP, the federal government became aware of Spitzer's involvement with prostitutes due to a wiretap. Following the public disclosure of his actions, Spitzer resigned as Governor effective March 17, 2008.
†Elizabeth Edwards was an American attorney, author, and health care activist, married to John Edwards, the former U.S. Senator from North

Indeed, the way Elizabeth Edwards was attacked was extraordinary; the attacks included everything from accusing Edwards of conspiring with her wicked husband to mislead the public to her attitude towards his mistress, culminating in a magnificently nasty piece written by Kathleen Parker for the online publication *The Daily Beast*, in which she remarked that "… wise women know that the world's Elizabeths owe the world's Hunters a thank-you note." In the wildly vituperative context of Parker's essay the comment was almost a non sequitur, and message-board commenters could make no sense of it. On the face of it, I think Parker flippantly meant to say that women married to cads ought to be thankful to the single predators out there for taking the worthless bastards off their hands—but on a more murky visceral level, it felt like a particularly hard slap in Elizabeth's face: as the "good woman" she was actually being instructed to thank the "bad woman," who traditionally would be pilloried in the public square while the wife looked on with satisfaction. In this case, not only was the mistress getting a free pass—I saw nothing criticizing Rielle Hunter—but for God's sake, the damn *wife* was in the stocks. As I read Parker's screed, along with dozens like it, I asked myself, What is going on here?

*

Perhaps it should be obvious: adultery is a social threat that arouses raw anger and fear which the bellicose then need to discharge rather than merely feel, traditionally most savagely on the adulteress or the home-wrecker. Monogamy is the religiously

Carolina who was the 2004 United States Democratic vice-presidential nominee. She separated from her husband following revelations of his extra-marital affair with Rielle Hunter, and wrote two books about her life: *Saving Graces* and *Resilience*.

undergirded ideal for nearly every culture on the planet (even polygamous cultures expect monogamy from women) and yet for centuries, men were unfaithful and tolerated as such, as long as they kept it quiet, and respected their wives as opposed to the mistresses or prostitutes they dallied with. It is a good thing, or at least a fair thing, in modern life that fidelity is expected on both sides. It is good too, or at least realistic, that sexually independent women have been given a degree of acceptance in the form of playfully sexual pop icons, respect for unmarried single moms and acknowledgement of women's sexual feelings in portrayals such as those in, say, *Sex and the City*.

But fair and realistic can also be confusing. If men are expected to be monogamous too (even if it seems they still are less likely to be), that means everybody has to be good all the time and that is hard, especially in a floridly sexual and permissive climate. Monogamy is desirable for many reasons, especially in terms of creating a stable, emotionally connected home for children. But judging from centuries of human behavior, it is also a very difficult standard to meet. Women seem to be more inclined to it than men, but I doubt that is because we are more moral. I think it is because if women have children their erotic/emotional energy is very taken up by that in a way that men's traditionally is not. And it seems to me that morality is not always the issue. Or rather, that total fidelity can come with a moral price tag of its own.

What is faithfulness anyway? Can you be unfaithful to your own feelings and be faithful to someone else? Is it faithful to lie in bed night after night with someone you love but no longer desire, while ardently dreaming of someone else? Is it faithful to make love to your wife while lewdly fantasizing about someone else again and again? Is it faithful to be monogamous if that means deadening your own nature, constantly, in order to be genitally true to someone you may love but no longer have physical passion for? For two people to satisfy everything each needs for their entire lives is a tall order. Some couples may be equipped to do this. Some are not.

In "The Marriage of Heaven and Hell," the poet William Blake said "Sooner strangle an infant in its crib than nurse an unacted desire." Maybe he meant, don't nurse it, kick it to the curb! But given the poem's joyous mash-up of hellish and holy, it seems more likely that Blake meant to honor desire and its many forms of expression; whatever he meant in terms of action, the line speaks eloquently of the tension between the pure quality of desire versus the forces of propriety that would contain it.

And how great that tension when you live in a society where well-bred teenagers with words like "juicy" written in pink script across their butts drive around in the car daddy bought them with "Porn Star" stamped on their license plates, with Lady Gaga on the radio singing about "bluffin' with my muffin." In other words, a society that is sexually hyper-stimulated all the time, yet fiercely values monogamy and fidelity in marriage. Adultery causes heart-break—and yet men and women do it every day because they feel it would break their spirit not to. It's a problem, and everybody knows it. That is why Anna Karenina and Madame Bovary are great heroines, and why adultery is a soap opera staple. That is also why adultery in high-profile people, especially elected officials whose job it supposedly is to be good all the time, brings out an especially nasty asexual desire—that is the desire to stone someone in the public square, or to at least pillory their hypocritical ass.

This desire is acted out on adulterers most vigorously: Eliot Spitzer lost his job and his honor; Mark Sanford* is in danger of

---

*Former governor of South Carolina and a former member of the U.S. House of Representatives. In June 2009, after having disappeared from the state for nearly a week, Sanford publicly revealed that he had engaged in an extramarital affair. Sanford had led his staff to believe that

losing both; Bill Clinton, an exception all his life, barely squeaked by with both sort of intact, even if he was impeached. The much despised John Edwards will never make a successful run for higher office. "Cad," "heel," "hypocrite," and "narcissist" were some of the nicer things said about these men in papers of note; limitless and merciless scorn was heaped upon them via the internet, where it was suggested by an anonymous poster that Edwards ought to be "hung up by his mistress's favorite part of him."

I feel an impulse to defend these men on the perhaps lax grounds that none of us know why they acted as they did, what their personal circumstances really are or what anguish they experienced—it's hard for me to imagine they experienced none. Their crimes were ordinary crimes of the heart which many everyday people commit without being subject to such punishment. Their hypocrisy is practically a job requirement which we, in our hypocrisy, demand of them.

And yet my impulse to defend them is tempered by the above-mentioned obvious: they broke a centuries-old moral code and in some cases used taxpayer's money to do it. If one wants to do that, one must be prepared to take the consequences, including vicious public scorn. But why have their wives been punished too? Think of it: would you want to be described, in print, over and over again, as "humiliated" by people—strangers, actually—who are supposedly taking your side? Even Jenny Sanford, who didn't attend her husband's press conference confession, and who read to me as more pissed off than shamed, was criticized by Tina Brown for failing to "rip off her burqa and revolt on behalf of all the other downtrodden political wives called to genuflect before their husbands' outsize egos." In other words, I guess, because she didn't chase Mr. Sanford down the street with a rolling pin.

---

he was going hiking on the Appalachian Trail, but actually went to visit his mistress Maria Belén Chapur in Argentina.

What is humiliation exactly? People often use the word as if it is merely a particularly potent form of embarrassment, but to me it is something more extreme. By it, I mean that a person's image of themselves has been debased, not only before others, but in their own hearts. The first dictionary definition is perhaps less dire: it means the loss of pride, self-respect or dignity. These words in their most authentic sense refer more to internal states than to how one is seen by others. Using any of these definitions, is it right to *automatically* describe the wives of adulterers as humiliated? Why? The wrongful act was committed by their husbands, not them. Why must they be said to have lost pride or self-respect because of the actions of someone close to them? It isn't surprising if they are embarrassed, anyone might feel that way about the kind of scrutiny they have been subjected to. But why should we announce that a woman has lost her dignity because her husband slept with someone else? Shouldn't she be the judge of that? Or do we actually believe that her dignity is entirely dependent on how men or even one man relates to her? Is she "humiliated" because she has failed to be all things to her husband, all the time, in perpetuity, at least as far as he is concerned—in other words because she has failed to do the impossible? (Or simply because she has failed to be beautiful enough; America Online posted a picture of Tiger Woods' gorgeous blond wife with the caption "Who would cheat on *her*?," a piece of stupidity that needs no comment.) It seems a curious form of emotional brutality to insist that a person must feel a certain way and then to repeatedly define them that way in public—if everyone is insisting that you are humiliated, how much harder to know what you actually feel.

Elizabeth Edwards was of course subjected to worse than this punitive definition: the real outrage came when she published her book—that is, when she tried to define herself. The anger was supposedly because 1) Mrs. Edwards had supported her husband's run for the presidency even though she knew about the affair

2) because she said that, aside from the affair, she had a "perfect marriage" 3) that she was "cashing in" on the whole thing. But it seems to me that, like any loyal and ambitious wife, she'd been pointed at her husband's goal for decades and that it would've been hard to change direction with any speed, especially if she was feeling exhausted from living with a deadly illness. Yes, "the perfect marriage" sounds ridiculous—but doesn't anyone recognize in it a sort of stunned gallantry? Can anyone really think she needs the money all that badly? I believe her real motive for writing the book and speaking about it was to show the world and her children that her misfortune had *not* defined her. Of course the more you say that *whatever* doesn't define you, the more it does. But can she be blamed for trying?

*

It is necessary to remember in all this that the cuckold has also been a traditional object of snickering sympathy—unless he does the manly thing and physically punishes his wife, possibly by murdering her, which is sanctioned by law in some countries. I wonder if we will ever see a high-profile female adulterer in politics and if so, how *that* would be dealt with in the public square. I imagine that while the tenor of it would be different, the husbands too would be endlessly described as "humiliated" and that instead of committing murder, they too would content themselves with writing books. But do they *have* to be described that way? Who made this a rule of the game? Do all of us have to play by it, all the time? What is in it for us?

*

There *is* such a thing as humiliation through sexual betrayal of course, and I don't mean to pretend otherwise. When passion is alive and joined with love, it is the closest thing to sacred on earth, whether it takes place in marriage or not. When one lover loses this passion, it feels shocking and belittling to the one still engaged. And yet ... I can't prove it, but it seems to me that most of the time in marriage when one partner loses that passionate engagement, it's mutual, or quickly becomes that way. Sexual passion of the kind I have just described is short-lived by nature. Phrases like "you have to work to keep it going" are commonplace now. But while passion may reignite, it seems to do so on its own terms; it doesn't come when you call. Even more difficult: certain kinds of passion don't flourish in the daily-ness of domestic life, but depend on mystery, illusion and risk. Passion is sometimes completely incompatible with politeness or dignity in the normal *social* sense of the words.

This kind of passion may be called immoral or immature, but passion doesn't care—it doesn't come *where* you call it either. And if it doesn't, how can it be surprising if, after years or decades of its absence, one spouse, longing to feel that powerful life force again, not only gets interested in someone else, but gives him or herself over to it? The danger is anguish for everyone involved, and morality exists in part as protection against that kind of pain. However, there is such a thing as being so protected that your life begins to feel lifeless and rote.

Maybe we are so eager to seize on public figures who have been caught "cheating" and hold them up for outraged examination because we are secretly hoping for some kind of insight as to how we might avoid their fate. But the emotional truth of what they've done and why they've done it can't be said in the crude language of public discourse—language like "if you take out this piece ... I have a perfect marriage." Language like that is suitable for the public world of politics, not for what goes on between married people during the intimate, vulnerable realities of adultery and its aftermath—one possible reality being that working through the infidelity and the reasons it happened may bring them closer. Or not. In any case, they have to figure it out in their own way just as we do, in private. No matter how many interviews we read or see, how many pictures or videos, how many tell-alls get written, we will never see into the private circumstances of the Edwards, the Sanfords or the Spitzers, nor should we. We have enough to do trying to understand and know ourselves, if we could only stop bellowing about other people long enough to try.

And if we can't stop bellowing about the adulterers, can we at least maybe lay off their wives?

2010

Learning to Ride

I learned how to ride horses when I was 56. This was totally unexpected. At the time I lived right next to a stable in upstate New York, that is to say, horse country. But I never felt the strong attraction that some girls have for horses; I never felt any attraction at all. On the contrary I found their faces and body language—unlike that of cats or dogs—completely unreadable, which made their size, power and beauty flat-out unnerving if not frightening. I understood their glamour as well as the ranking and compeition that went with it—but for me the whole point of an animal companion was not glamour; I wanted to be soft and cuddly with a pet. I could see no way to cuddle with something as enormous and hard-bodied as a horse, and the idea of sitting atop a muscular thousand-pound creature without that soft channel of communication—that was not my idea of fun. It was not my idea of fun at 56 either. Yet there I was, atop a huge muscular creature with whom I was very uncomfortable and who didn't seem very happy with me either.

This unexpected thing happened because I had become passionately taken with the idea that I must write a book about a disadvantaged young girl who learns to ride against great odds.

Unexpected too was the timing of this idea: my marriage had broken up and my sister's marriage had also broken up right as she was becoming terribly ill. My 16-year-old goddaughter had become pregnant with a 35-year-old man's child. My unhappiness during this time was inter-cut with hope that took the form of sudden surges of feeling and imagery that would come into my head with the force of waking dreams: almost fully realized scenes of the girl and the horse, complete with dialogue. These mental images would come to me when I was in an airport worrying about a delayed flight or driving to the store or preparing to teach a class. They were often so emotionally loaded that my hair would stand up on my arms: I couldn't tell if I were losing my mind or having a transfiguring inspiration.

In an attempt to find out, I showed up at the stable next door which was run by a working-class mother-daughter team in their mid-80s (Cate) and mid-50s (Glenda). Both of them were big and rough in appearance, with broad sun-reddened faces and sharp, candid blue eyes; both were funny and plain spoken. I stood before them with my hair up, wearing silky summer clothes with pink high heels. Glenda looked me up and down and said "You remind me of, what's her name, Zsa-Zsa? The one trying to be a farmer in Green Acres?" I thought: maybe just a few lessons, two or four or six. Just enough to get a feel for it.

Except I couldn't. I was still reflexively looking for that soft "cuddle" connection which, completely apart from the horses, was not part of Cate or Glenda's vocabulary. While grooming a horse before saddling her, I would be trying to find the mare's "sweet spot," the place she would like being brushed. "Don't bother with that," Glenda would say curtly. "She doesn't care about that, she's saying, 'let's get to work.'" Glenda and Cate both emphasized the need to be strong with the animals, to be "in control." However, they also said that you could not fake anything with horses, that they would see it instantly. Which put me in a difficult position as I did not feel qualified to be "in control;" if it wasn't possible to at least pretend otherwise, that left me feeling pretty powerless.

This was not a feeling I was used to. Although I hated gym class and team sports when I was a kid, from my 20s on I'd found ways to be physical: martial arts, dancing, bike riding, long walks and weights at the gym. At 56 I was relatively fit and strong—but that didn't seem to matter as soon as I got on a horse, where I had to coordinate my legs and hands (and therefore my brain) in a way that was completely unfamiliar to me. It's one thing to press a weight with your inner thigh. It's a whole *other* thing to press against a live creature, to convey *intention* with your inner thigh, and to do it compellingly when the creature has a foreign and unpredictable mind of its own.

Every time I went to the stable for a lesson, or even just to groom horses or clean stalls (I was also helping out on a volunteer basis), I felt weak, scared and hopelessly inept, humiliatingly so in comparison with the confident young women who also rode there. (I remember one incident in particular when I was grooming a beautiful Icelandic gelding named Andrew; he began pawing and rearing on the cross-ties, and while I cowered against the wall, ready to cry out "Glenda!"—a passing teenager stopped, put her hands on her hips and shouted at him "Stand like a gentleman!" And he did.) Cate, who knew that I taught writing on a college level, would try to coach me by saying things like "Treat them like you treat your students—don't put up with any shit!" This was of no help: my confidence and authority with students—my confidence and authority, period—comes primarily from written and spoken language. It was not an authority that impressed the horses one bit—or, it seemed, Glenda and Cate who were, I suspect, secretly mystified that such a strange, timid person could get through life at all, let alone excel in a challenging field.

I had a particularly discouraging experience with a gelding

64

named Midnight, a lovely Tennessee Walker with an even dispo-sition. Because of his disposition, Glenda wanted me to ride him; he was boarded at the stable by a woman who never came to see him, but as he wasn't Glenda's horse, she didn't typically use him for lessons. She thought he would like me because I might remind him of a "little blond girl" who used to ride him, a girl he had become fond of. But it didn't work that way. I was used to riding a pony named Royalle, and in comparison, Midnight was very tall and narrow-bodied, which felt precarious to me. His stride was longer and his gait much stronger; the first time he went into a running walk, I was startled and pulled on his mouth too hard which made him toss his head and jog restively which scared me. I couldn't make him do much of anything for the entire lesson, and I never wanted to get on him again.

The feeling, it seemed was mutual. Some time after this lesson, I was leading Midnight out to the paddock to graze and he shoved me with his head, not hard enough to knock me down, but hard enough to make me stumble. Later, on a different day, as I was leading him back into his stall, he bolted in past me so fast that he knocked me into the wall. Dammit, I thought, even the *nice* horse here is pushing me around. Meanwhile, some months in, I was still not using my hands right and was still so tense that I tended to contract and hunch instead of fully extending my legs to push my heels into the stirrups, which is necessary for grounding. I was still nervous and uncomfortable in the saddle, which made any horse I sat on nervous and uncomfortable.

I decided to try another place, and it was there that I had my first break-through. Sort of. It happened on a cold day in early winter when I saw an elegant young girl student trotting around the arena bare-back. I asked the trainer if I could try it, just to see what it felt like. She was surprised, but she agreed. I got on the horse with nothing but a saddle-pad between me and him and—he felt *wonderful*, warm and so alive that my legs, all up and down them, came alive in reply. It was like a wild, intense form of *cuddling*, so astonishingly great that for a minute I forgot to be nervous. After walking around the arena a few times, the trainer asked if I wanted to go back to the saddle and I said no, let's stay with this. And I did stay with it, even when the horse unexpectedly broke into a trot (probably I unwittingly signaled him to do so) and it took me several long seconds to stop him. "Great work!" said the trainer.

That was the "break-through." Next came the "sort of." Because I had stayed on the horse even at a trot, I decided I would learn to trot bare-back; I made it to the second lesson before I fell off. I wasn't thrown off, I just fell. When I realized I was going to fall I tried to do a "quick dismount" and I got off light, with a cut chin and a pulled muscle in my back. Still, the fall made my fear return in a nauseating rush and I refused to get back on. For the next few days I felt like I'd been hit by a truck and the pulled muscle took a long time to heal. I tried to remember the wonderful feeling of the horse on my legs, but all I could think was: *If I keep this up I am going to break my dumb ass.* I went back to grooming and cleaning at Glenda's place—no riding.

It was a defeat but it was also freeing. I was teaching and writing, and physical labor at the barn was a welcome antidote to the mental labor, as well as to the emotional rawness I felt about everything that was going wrong. As long as I didn't have to ride them, I liked caring for the horses: brushing them, rubbing them, scratching them on their "sweet spots." After a few months, when I was working alone with Cate, I overheard her on the phone talking to a woman who boarded her horse there: "I'm almost done, Mary's here helping me ... yeah, that's the writer. No, no, they don't give her any trouble. She's got this real quiet way with them and they just go with her. No, even Cool Cat doesn't give her trouble." It was then that I regained the confidence to start riding again.

Then too came the second break-through, no "sort of." I was on Royalle when, without trying, I *felt her* on both my legs. By that I don't mean that I felt her body; it was more that I felt her being. It was a quick flash but it was delicious, gentle and *round*, not in its physical dimensions, but in its essence. Glenda quietly said "The mare's eyes just got soft," and I felt my body fully extended, heels down in the stirrups.

Then came another kind of break-through. Cate had told me that her son (Glenda's brother) was dying and that it was possible that one day I might come to the barn to find that they weren't there. She told me that in that event, they had someone who would feed and water the horses, that I should just take care of the animals I was responsible for. A few days later, that is what happened. I did my job while the horses all looked at me anxiously, wondering, I suppose, where their main ladies were. Royalle's was the last stall I cleaned. Right next to her was Midnight. Normally, he would ignore me while I cleaned, but that day he stood stock still, staring at me fixedly, sometimes even turning his head so he could look at me with one eye and then the other. Clearly, he was trying to tell me something, so I went around to the other side of the barn to look into his stall. It was absolutely filthy. His mute face said "help me" so plainly it was as if he had spoken the words.

I didn't speak out loud. But I thought at him: *I would like to help, but I'm afraid of you. You shoved me with your head and then you knocked me against the wall.* He continued to stare at me and again, I understood as plainly as if he'd spoken: *I'm not going to hurt you. I need help. Please help.*

And so I went into his stall and cleaned it. It is generally a much better idea to take the horse out of the stall to clean, especially if it's not a horse you're comfortable with. But because I'd had problems when I'd lead him, I felt better going in, at least after I'd put some hay in his bucket to get him away from the door. As soon as I entered, I realized I was safe. I cleaned one side of the stall, then gently pushed him to the other side and cleaned that. When I was done I stood with him and stroked his neck. His lips trembled with pleasure; I felt a flood of happiness. This was not exactly cuddling, but I never felt more connected with an animal than at that moment.

I didn't expect to ride Midnight after that. But I did start cleaning his stall and grooming him, and when I did those things, I felt a milder version of the same connection. Then one day Glenda said to me "I have a very special request for you. You don't have to accept it, but it is a request." She paused. I listened. She said "Midnight really, really wants you to ride him." I looked at the horse. He looked at me, inclining his head, all but batting his eyelashes. It was unbelievably sweet and so was the ride. His stride was still very strong; even with his mild personality, his energy was more intense than Royalle's. But I was more experienced and knew how to be easier on his mouth. When I dismounted and came around to his front to say "thank you," he pressed his nose against my cheek and held it there for a long moment.

I rode only him after that, long trail rides I would take with Glenda. I also sometimes took him out to exercise him on a "lunge-line," and then walked around with him letting him graze. When summer came I bathed him. Sometimes I would just go into his stall and put my arms around him; he would drape his head on my shoulder. I had no fear of him, even though once he got snotty during a lunging session and yanked me off my feet. Because he was a gaited horse and didn't trot under saddle I stopped learning how to ride at a trot. I didn't care, I didn't want to ride anyone but him.

After about a year I accepted a two-semester position as a "visting writer" four hours drive away; a furnished house came with the job and so I put all my stuff in storage, put my cat in the car and left. I found another stable in my new "home" and continued to take lessons there, mostly on a business-like Paint horse named Buzz. I made no emotional connection with Buzz, but he was a well-trained lesson horse and he had a wonderful smooth stride that was perfect for me. My posture became better, my inner legs stronger and more *intelligent* as I finally learned how to trot. Eventually, I began cantering, and the first time I really *got it*, a huge smile broke out over my face. I was still scared and uncomfortable at times but mostly I felt satisfied and exhilerated at the end of a lesson. And my book was almost done.

But I did not forgot Midnight. Every month I would make the drive down to see him, to trail ride him or just take him out to exercise and graze. At the end of the year I planned to move to New York City which was close enough for me to come visit Midnight regularly. I fantasized about buying him. At least I thought things could be the same as they had been.

They weren't. When I went back I found out that Glenda and Cate had very nearly gone out of business. They'd relocated, with very few horses, in their backyard. They had only two or three boarders left. I had one more reunion with Midnight before his owner decided she didn't want to board him with Glenda anymore. In the years I had been coming to the stable, I had not seen this woman once; Glenda said she *never* even came to see her horse, let alone ride him. But one day she came and took him away. And I never saw him again.

I finished my book, but I never became a good rider. I just barely learned to canter and I never really jumped. If I'd been able to keep it up with Midnight I would've, even if it had to be on another horse. But without him I lost interest. My time with him was lovely and invaluable; I miss him as I would miss a person. I believe I have kept some of the benefits of riding, in terms of confidence and leg-awareness—but I recall Midnight and the feeling-qualities of that time much more vividly than I do the skills required to ride. Even now, in New York City on my own, I might be sitting on the subway or in a crowded restaurant when I will suddenly remember Glenda's barn early in the morning, the smells and sounds of the horses, their warmth; the feeling of Midnight's head on my shoulder, or his body under me. I remember how vulnerable and inadequate I felt to the task, and how I did it anyway. It is a melancholy feeling but it is strengthening too. I remember Glenda admonishing me to keep my heels grounded and my intention clear. And in a different way, wherever I am, I try to do exactly that. I just wish I still had Midnight to do it with.

Watching and Listening

I've Seen It All: Thoughts on a Song by Björk

Most soundtrack albums exist completely separately from the movies they're attached to because the songs selected already have a vital popular character that the movie has borrowed to enhance itself, and this rarely works the other way around. The exception is the old-fashioned musical—and that is what Lars von Trier's *Dancer in the Dark* is, sort of. This "sort of" applies in different ways to both the film and Björk's album of the same name, the movie because, instead of simply being a musical, it is self-consciously *about* musicals, and the album because it appropriates the genre in a somewhat tedious postmodern way. However, both the movie and the album have power that is wholly unique, almost secret, and it comes from the way the play off each other. Specifically it shows up in one astonishingly beautiful song called "I've Seen It All" which makes the CD worthwhile. The song amplifies the meaning of the film, even surpasses it in elucidating what seems to me *Dancer*'s most powerful theme. Yet the song couldn't really exist without the movie.

Dancer in the Dark is ostensibly about an oppressed factory worker named Selma (played by Björk), who is going blind and who is saving every hard-earned penny to buy an operation for her son in order to save him from this congenital condition. Her money is stolen by a loathsome cop who has pretended to be her friend, who then weirdly (unbelievably, you might say) insists that she shoot him. She complies, then gives the money to the eye surgeon, is betrayed, caught and executed. Meanwhile, in her fantasies, everyone sings and dances.

Like von Trier's *Breaking the Waves*, this is a story of transfiguring agony experienced by a child-like innocent. In the earlier film, the heroine's masochistic sexual sacrifice, supposedly made to save her husband, makes emotional sense because of the intense mystical relationship von Trier built between the two characters. But, in *Dancer*, he has Selma sacrificing herself for her child, and yet the child barely exists. She appears more involved with her imaginary musicals and seems absolutely indifferent to her son's emotional well-being. Neither the devotion of her best friend (played by Catherine Deneuve) nor the malevolent cop quite makes sense, at least as they are portrayed. However, in a deeper, stranger sense, *Dancer* is the more powerful film, its real force being an undercurrent that has only a refracted relationship to the supposed story. That force is derived not from the story of sacrifice, but from an ecstatic spiritual underpinning that includes the transcendence of character and plot.

This is where von Trier's genius shows itself: in making music so important in the film, and in choosing a pop singer with a forceful, otherworldly persona to be his star, he seems to understand that his irrational, ecstatic theme is better served by voice and sound than by story. In this light, the musical sequences are not just charming, weird delusions, they are there to show that under the "story" of these lives there is a broader reality in which people who are deadly enemies or dear friends are merely playing roles almost for the sake of the soul's exercise. Further, these roles are in fact flimsy and can be stepped out of for transcendent moments that expose human personality as a mask and human

74

action, whether compassionate or cruel, as a kind of ridiculous theater. For example, after Selma shoots the cop, he gets up off the floor and they sing together; he understands that she merely, as the lyrics say, "did what [she] had to do." In this context, Selma is not an innocent, she is a blind "seer" who understands all this through music in a way that the people around her do not. As a story, the movie fails this material because, if it is about the illusion of "character" and "plot" in human life, then paradoxically its own plot and characters need to be highly developed and believable illusions, not hastily constructed cut-outs. But "I've Seen It All" very nearly redeems this failure, almost making the film and the soundtrack into a hybrid art form, and hinting at a way of creating stories through combinations of different media.

In the movie, the song is sung by Selma and a man with a hopeless crush on her who has realized she is going blind and confronted her with it. He pleads with her to get an operation to restore her sight, and she says she has no need to see anymore. They are on a train track when a train roars by; suddenly they are on the train itself, singing as they speed past domestic tableaux, while rail workers do balletic routines. It's essentially a love song of renunciation and it is very tender. The man lists all the things she will miss seeing, and she answers with what she *has* seen. "You've never been to Niagara Falls? / I've seen water—it's water, that's all." It's about outer abundance—all the great stuff like Niagara—versus the inner abundance that comes from being able to see what is right before you. The song opens and contracts; smallness becomes bigness, the man's idea of big becomes small, and then you can't tell which is which.

On the album, the actor is replaced by Thom Yorke of Radiohead, and he and Björk share the roles so that sometimes it is she who interrogates him. (That makes sense in the song because it doesn't matter which character is answering or asking, it is the exultant feel of expansion and contraction, of acknowledgment and release.) Without the visual aspect, the song is stripped-down and childishly simple, with Seuss-like lyrics and a monotonous industrial back-beat. It is also lush, expansive, emotionally complex. Björk's voice goes from crumpled, nearly retarded, to wide and powerful as a highway to heaven. Yorke's voice, sometimes rhetorically sentimental yet giving full honor to sentiment, has never been more beautiful or nuanced. He can also sound like a righteous therapist. When she asks, in the voice of a pinched imp, "What about China? Have you seen the Great Wall?" he answers "All walls are great if the roof doesn't fall," and he seems nearly too pleased with this bit of wisdom. But the stuck-up part is tonally cut with a gentleness that gets fully expressed on that last word, "fall." When he asks, "Your grandson's hand as he plays with your hair?" his voice describes sorrowful tenderness in so many shades you can't parse it. And so she answers with singsong insouciance that is almost bratty: "To be honest, I really don't care." And then the music opens out like sky and Björk's voice opens even more, in an electric combination of pain and joy—because almost any woman would care. Her joy is that of a person with so little joy in her life that she's been forced to find it where she can, and both singers seem to understand this. "I've seen it all, I've seen the dark, / I've seen the brightness in one little spark." Both voices sing this line in a duet, *West Side Story* style, and together they give reality to lyrics that, taken strictly at face value, could be New Age treacle.

In fact, I've quoted lyrics here mainly to locate particular shifts in the song; it's the voices and music, not the lyrics, that mark these shifts most effectively. It's the voices and music that convey the mystery, the transient changeability of human feeling, better than the movie. The song creates a sense of beauty and abundance that the struggling movie characters, with their small lives, would not seem entitled to, yet which they can not only possess through the strength of their inner abundance, but which they can also refuse. Because the song itself is finally a refusal, one that acknowledges the beauty of all it refuses—holding it, then letting it go.

It's also, more simply, a powerful example of what's populist in "pop"—its lovely ordinariness. "I've Seen It All" is a passionate evocation of what is great in ordinary people, with their crummy jobs and fantasies, people who are not even supposed to "have a life." When I interviewed Radiohead some time ago, bassist Ed O'Brien said pop songs are like snapshots meant to be thrown away the next day. That is very true. But in the sense suggested by "I've Seen It All," that is also true of everything human. And I mean that in a good way.

2001

Remain In Light: On the Talking Heads

Lost my shape—trying to act casual!
Can't stop—I might end up in the hospital
                          —"Cross-eyed and Painless"
                          Talking Heads, *Remain in Light*

In 1979 I was an almost total dork. I didn't know what was going on—in any way, really, but especially as regards culture and fashion.

My first encounter with culture and fashion was when I was seven and my mother took us to a roller skating rink, where teenagers wearing 'dos and poodle skirts with flannel appliqués roared ferociously around in a circle while music played. One girl's skirt had on it slogans like "Do The Twist!" and "The Mashed Potato!" and I watched her ferocious movement around the rink with amazement and terror.

I was afraid because I was looking at a world of signifiers and abstraction, broad basic swatches of feeling and experience expressed in symbols that were both general and refined, a whole language of symbols that I didn't speak and which instantly struck me as too complex to learn. I was looking at the future.

Five years later, I would be required, along with everyone else in my junior high school, to fit my personality into a similar system of symbols that I couldn't get right. The only thing that kept me from social autism was music. Anything from Nancy Sinatra to the Four Tops to Mitch Ryder to The Association—it was refined and shapely like the social styles that so defeated me, but it was also fluid and fundamental as pre-verbal sound. The songs did not have prescribed meaning for me, so they could mean anything. I would go to sleep at night with my transistor radio pressed against my head, letting the "anything" take forms that were too mysterious and personal to turn into a symbol that I could put on my skirt or my hair. It made me feel connected, even to the people who had mastered the art of style—because I understood in some way that they must hear this more mysterious thing too.

Three years later I dropped out of school and ran away from home. For a while it was like disappearing into the songs on the radio. But in five years I was struggling to get by, and by then I wasn't paying attention to any style system. I liked music a lot, but it was background to me, not any kind of main event. I liked Patti Smith, The Cars, 10CC, The Electric Light Orchestra, Robin Trower, Roxy Music, and it was all equal to me. It did not have prescribed meaning, and it did not define me in any way. When I decided to go back to school, I went to community college and hung out with people who got high in deserted housing developments and screwed to Frampton's Camel, then drove home meditating on Gary Wright's "Dream Weaver." I liked that too.

Then I went to a real University and met people who knew what was going on. I briefly went out with a guy I'll call Jenkins who introduced me to the Ramones, Elvis Costello and the Talking Heads. He had excellent taste. He read *Rolling Stone* and the *Village Voice* and he knew exactly what these bands meant and why they were important. He and his friends had a softball team called The Psycho Killers (with individual shirts labeled "Ted Bundy," "Richard Speck" etc.) and *Texas Chainsaw Massacre* posters up in their house. It was like being at the roller rink. It was also like pressing the transistor radio to my ear. I didn't know how to separate the music from the pretense around it—college-kid pretense, both wonderful and idiotic, a mixture that felt so false and so true that I didn't know how to react to it. Like a dork I would fume about snotty art students singing songs about murder—*I* had experienced *real* violence, I said, and it wasn't funny. But I said that because I didn't know how to say what I really felt—which was that the cleverness, humor and sometimes perverse torque of the music was a near flawless form that I felt stunned by and locked out of.

I still don't know what was going on in 1979. What I remember is a mass dream of joy and pain, both slightly delirious, neither fully felt. The non-feeling created a certain morbid innocence that in my mind looks like that of the victims in the disaster/ murder movies that were popular then—an awful blank optimism, best expressed on the "face" of "Mr. Bill," the cartoon victim on *Saturday Night Live*. Jenkins was right, "Psycho Killer" was the perfect song for this moment. And because it was he who was right, the music got mixed up with sex that was like twisting and crushing myself into weird forms until my "self" broke and something powerful and formless came out, then withdrew again.

I heard that in the music, too; the weird, twisting form, the bouncing, jerking, deliberate and sophisticated childishness of it. I loved it and hated it. Maybe I felt mocked by it. The week Jenkins and I broke up I published a story in a local paper about a hydrocephalic guy in a wheelchair who'd been wrongfully locked up in a state home for (to speak in the cruel tongue of that time) crazy retarded people because his inner-city family was poor and battered to pieces. It got bounced out of the lead position by a million-word analysis of how important the Ramones were. There was a huge picture of the Ramones joyfully pretending to be retards while the deformed beatific face of the hydrocephalic guy smiled from the corner. It was me and the hydrocephalic guy vs. Jenkins and the Ramones and they'd won! I felt like the fool David Byrne sings "No Compassion" at, and it was more humiliating than it should have been.

Or maybe it was exactly like it should've been. It was around then that I started waking up in the morning and having no idea who I was or where I was. I had to remind myself, and it took several minutes. I would call up images, pictures of myself doing things: walking to class, in a restaurant drinking tea, talking to someone. At first the pictures were bizarre and alien, then neutral, then I'd say, oh, right, and get out of bed. Myself, it seemed, really had broken, and something unfamiliar was trying to emerge. It was scary, but it was powerful too. I wanted to know who it was that was looking at the pictures before I said "oh, right." I started writing stories that were more real than anything I had written before. I started listening to music, really listening. Sometimes I wrote with headphones on.

It was during this time that I heard *Remain in Light*. It was like meeting an enemy and realizing he's an ally. It was like the hard, clever form of their old songs had burst, and something was pouring out of it—something that had always been there. Listening was like going through a tiny door and coming out somewhere vast, with thousands of doors and windows to a thousand other places. Sometimes the music flew past the places, and sometimes through them. One world might be the gauze through which you looked at another, and then it would be the world. I could be the person walking down the street or having tea and then I could be the person looking and not knowing who I was; each moved through the other, seen and not seen. I was changing shape, and it was an accident, and this music not only understood that, it celebrated it. It described something that was happening in me, and something that was happening in the world, all the time, to the hydrocephalic guy and to psycho killer.

I wasn't saying this to myself while I listened to the music. It was something I understood deeper than words, in a way my mind could only glimpse. The understanding was like a seed and it would be a long time before it began to germinate. It would be even longer before I had the means to communicate what was being grown. But that was okay. I knew it was there. I heard it.

2003

Imaginary Light: A Song Called "Nowhere Girl"

I don't know why this song touched me. I heard it at a small Manhattan club in '81; it came tingling through the crowded dark and lightly touched me with an indefinable feeling that was intense almost *because* it was so light—and then disappeared into whatever song followed. It was in no way the best song I heard during that time; it did not "save me." I did not even go out and buy it, though if I'd been able to afford anything to play it on, I might've. *Might've.* I am not a fan by nature and it was a slight, slightly ridiculous song. But it touched me in a way I could not quite forget. I heard it randomly maybe three more times; I didn't go out that much and apparently it wasn't hugely popular. But each time I heard it, it touched me in that peculiarly light and emotional way, with the quality of something small that is trying to get your attention, though unconfidently, from somewhere off in a corner. Or from nowhere.

"Nowhere girl in self-imposed exile / Nowhere girl in martyr-like denial." Part of what touched me was the word "nowhere," and the idea of someone living there, a picture of mysteriously seductive loneliness, a delicate and melancholy thing expressed in manic synth-pop. (Maybe it unconsciously reminded me of a fantasy story I'd written when I was fifteen, in which some space-traveling teenagers come across a beautiful woman confined in a transparent false world that moves fluidly with her movements, in which she lives a hallucinatory non-life, unaware of "real world" people who can watch her delusional existence but who cannot help her.) "Nowhere girl, you've never gone outside / Nowhere girl cause you prefer to hide / Every day, every night, in that old familiar light": the words "everyday" and "light" activated this phrase, and, put together with the music, made multiple pictures that blended and flashed through me. Everyday light: light in a basement, streetlight, club light, imaginary light; something as mundane as a lamp and as sinister as the glow of a hypnotizing dream that the girl has become lost in, yet which is at the same time the only thing keeping her alive. The music evokes delight, longing, urgent melancholy and fun: "And I try to get through / And I try to talk to you / But there's something stopping me from getting through." The sincere, slightly exasperated, actually pretty happy voice is that of a guy in cheap, fashionable clothes that look good as long as it's dark; he's no prince, and he's more bemused than ardent—still the song has the enchanted feeling of Sleeping Beauty, though in this case the enchantment will not break.

So much association and imagery is a lot of weight to put on such a small song, and I didn't think any of that at the time, I just felt it sort of speeding past. But the wistful sound that translated as a kind of emotional touch entered my system with all of that somehow encoded, and it bloomed in my subconscious imagination like the artificial sea shell somebody gave me when I was a kid which, when dropped into a glass of water, opened and bloomed into an elaborate flower.

This is a quality that many, maybe all good pop songs have, this deceptively light ability to touch and awaken multiple associations that blend with the wordless, innocent and completely non-hierarchical sense of dreams. (For someone else's fantastically rendered dream of this song, in a more tarted-up and sentimental version than the one I first heard, see the video posted by somebody called "davidapa" on YouTube; it's a beautiful mash-up with the mad scientist scene in Fritz Lang's *Metropolis*, in which the theme of awakening is demonically moving.) It's a quality that I felt more complexly in many other songs from the same time which I find better and more delicious, songs by Crime and the City Solution, Talking Heads, Joy Division, Roxy Music, Patti Smith, Sonic Youth, and the Psychedelic Furs among others. It is a quality that can make pop music appear ephemeral to the point of cheap, exceptionally vulnerable to changes in fashion, attachable to dumb things like ads for cars or pizza, dependent on its period of time for its language of shared associations to make sense. It is also a quality that makes pop music exceptionally powerful in its ability to enter a person's most private schema and whisper to that person in secret.

*

It makes sense that this song wasn't popular; what night-clubber in NYC wants to identify with some lonely loser sitting by herself in the basement, staring into space? At the same time, it also makes sense that this lonely loser and the guy trying to get her out of the basement appeared in NYC in 1981, a time of costuming, pretense, fancy-shaped, day-glo colored hair. Costuming is a romantic way of giving shape to something previously inchoate inside you, of trying to discover, to become. It can also be a way of obnoxiously parading the self while simultaneously hiding it, especially if the costume is socially agreed on. The song is about a person who "prefers to hide" in a physical place, such as a room, but also perhaps in the self, in a construction of personality in which something essential and vulnerable remains hidden and undeveloped. When I heard "Nowhere Girl," I was lost in a self-created nightmare that had become a terrible reality I was trying desperately to get out of, and instead was getting more lost in by the moment. I think the song in its quick passing gave me a strange glimmer of hope just because in it I could hear that other people saw and felt this lostness too, and rather than despising it, someone had considered it worth writing a song about.

By '86, I was starting to find my way. I could sort of talk to people. I remember, though, a particular moment when I couldn't. I was spending an afternoon with this guy I liked, and we were walking around doing something I no longer recall. I do remember that at one point we sat down outside somewhere and he said, "I really like you and I want to get to know you. But it feels like there's all these obstacles and I don't know what they are and I don't know how to get around them." I was so astonished that I could not reply. I knew exactly what he meant. At the same time, *I* didn't know what the obstacles were either. I crossed my hands over my lap and looked down. I have no idea what I was thinking. Maybe I was trying to come up with something smart to say and realizing that it was beyond me. Probably I thought he was saying there was something wrong with me. He put his hand on my arm, then took it away. The moment passed. We talked about something else, then said good-bye.

Because I knew I was going to write about this song, I told this anecdote to someone recently and she said, "It just sounds like he was coming on to you." My mind snagged on the word "just;" I seldom think that anyone "just" comes on. I don't know what he wanted or what he was doing. I remember the moment because I felt he was trying to get through, trying to talk to me, and that something was stopping him—and that yet, he succeeded. It is still moving to me that he saw something real that most people wouldn't bother to see, and that he said something about it; that he helped me, in a tiny way, to wake up.

By '87 I had gotten somewhere in the social sense; I had sold a book and it was about to be published. I remember going to a club for the first time in a while and being kind of appalled. There were no costumes, no sense of discovery or romance; there were mostly a lot of expensive clothes, and I was wearing them too. The best thing was the DJ, who for some reason made me remember a song I hadn't heard in years; I went up to her and asked, do you have "Nowhere Girl" by B Movie? She did. She played it and for a moment the room was drenched in feeling from the past: the feeling of something unknown trying to get your attention, of not quite being able to see what it is; of somebody trying to awaken somebody else; of trying to wake. Banal somewhere was suddenly and beautifully infused with mysterious nowhere. It was a very small moment, but it was a lovely one. As this is a small but lovely song.

2010

Victims and Losers, A Love Story: Thoughts on the Movie *Secretary*

In 1992 an inexperienced young director named Steven Shainberg first approached me about making a movie of *Secretary*, my story about a naïve young masochist who yearns for emotional contact in an autistic and ridiculous universe, and who winds up getting her butt spanked instead. Mr. Shainberg was very young and very earnest, and while he got the yearning, he didn't get the ridiculousness. He seemed bent on assuring me that he would not belittle Debby's suffering though I sought no such assurance. During one elaborate assurance he brought up the movie *Pretty Woman*, which, he said, had been ruined by Hollywood philistines. The original script was very dark and ended with the angrily screaming prostitute being dragged out of a car by her 3-day john and thrown on the sidewalk before he flies off to get married. He expressed outrage at the light and charming spin the movie had put on the innately painful and degrading subject; his indignation was so excessive that I actually felt roused to defend a film I didn't think much of. Yes, it was phony and insipid, but Hollywood is phony and insipid about housewives and mothers, and I wasn't especially indignant regarding this treatment of prostitutes, whom I didn't see as innately degraded. He seemed baffled and even offended. Ten years later he made the *Pretty Woman* version of my story.

*

The bare plot of *Secretary* the story could be the plot of a classic wank book: Hopeful Innocent takes a job as a secretary where she is abused, spanked and jerked off on by Mean Bossman. She is weeping and shamed, her face is as scarlet as her red-hot bottom—*and her pussy is dripping wet!* But life is dirtier than porn, and I didn't get the idea from a wank book. I got it out of the newspaper. It was a small story reprinted in the "No Comment" section of *Ms Magazine*, circa 1980, and it reported that, somewhere in the Midwest, a lawyer running for public office had been revealed to have abused his former secretary by spanking her and videotaping her standing in a corner repeating "I am stupid." On being revealed, he sought to make things right by apologizing and giving the woman $200. I'm sure *Ms* didn't intend it this way, but the blandly reported story, in addition to being ludicrous, had a great erotic charge, primarily because both players were faceless ciphers whom the imagination easily translated as archetypes. On reading it I laughed, then shook my head in dismay, then thought, what a great story—funny, horrible, poignant and gross, the misery of it as deep as the eroticism; the misery in fact giving the eroticism its most pungent force. The wank book aspect was clearly indispensable, but what interested me most was: who is this girl? The "hopeful innocent" in the porn story, the cipher in the news story—what would she be like in real life?

*

In any genuine piece of fiction, the plot is like the surface personality or external body of a human being; it serves to contain

89

the subconscious and viscera of the story. The plot is something you "see" with your rational mind, but the unconscious and the viscera—what you can smell and feel without being able to define—is the deeper subject of the story. This is particularly true of *Secretary*, the heroine of which is a knot of smothered passion expressed only obliquely and negatively in her outer self. I conceived her as someone of unformed strength and intelligence, which have never been reflected back to her by her world and so have become thwarted, angry and peculiar. The deeper subject of *Secretary* then, is the tension between the force and complexity inside the heroine, and how it gets squeezed through the tiny conduit of a personality which she has learned to make small so that she may live in the small and mute world around her. Debby's parents are not abusive, they are defeated—to some extent by the severely limited world around them, but primarily by their own emotional ineptitude. Their daughter's desire to humiliate herself may be accurately described as self-hatred; however, looked at less judgmentally, it's an ardent and truthful desire to represent, with her own being, the distorted world around her and inside her, where force and passion are humiliated and punished by being ignored or twisted. Debby's passivity is so willed and extreme that it is an act of mutually annihilating aggression; there can be no "relationship" with the boss, even if he were to desire one (which he does not), and questions about whether or not she is victimized by him are irrelevant. His only superiority is in his ability to recognize her—as one of his own kind. For her passion is every bit as cruel as his, and this is what is horrible in the story.

However, coexisting with all this is the yearning that Mr. Shainberg perceived from the beginning. Whatever else she may be, Debby is a sensitive girl acutely attuned to the emotional world. Hunger for contact underlies her perversity and to some extent drives it. Early in the story, she recalls an instant of loving touch from her sister, wistfully noting that such an instant has never occurred again. At the height of her experience with her boss, she has romantic dreams in which they walk together in a field of flowers, holding hands and smiling with "a tremendous sense of release and goodwill." One room away from her family, she longs for real connection with them, and the fear that she will never have it plunges her into despair. Her unformed aggression and cruelty are surpassed only by her unformed tenderness. What a shocking relief when, at work, both impulses are poetically expressed through emotionally violent and intense sex that occurs without touching. Simultaneously Debbie and "the lawyer" achieve total intimacy and total isolation, and this paradox is the heart of the story's anguish and harsh comedy. The character's ability to hold this paradox is the source of her dignity, even if she holds it unknowingly. Without understanding how, she is aware that she bears equal responsibility for what is happening. Given this awareness, when the reporter calls, urging her to expose her boss, what can she do but hang up?

*

This is an almost impossible story to make a movie of. Its drama is internal, rendered in language very nearly like code and meant to be sensed rather than explicitly seen. I admire Steven Shainberg for attempting it, and for succeeding to the extent that he did. It bears almost no relationship to the original story because it couldn't—not in America anyway, where *Belle du Jour* or *Repulsion* would now be met with either fear or blank incomprehension. For it to be commercially successful, a relationship between boss and girl needed to occur and so it does. To be successful, the relationship must end in marriage, and so it does. (Perhaps the most socially threatening thing about the story is that Boss Man is actually not very important.) Unlike Debby in the story, the movie heroine (played by Maggie Gyllenhaal and re-named Lee) has just been released from a mental hospital and is an anorexic self-mutilator. She is puppy-eyed and slump-shouldered, but this melancholy affect is oddly superficial; it is quickly neutralized by Lee's big, glowing smiles, which unmistakably signal the assurance and ease of a happy and loveably ditzy person. When the boss says to her "you're closed up, tight," it doesn't make sense because we're looking at a soft, receptive, essentially sunny face. When first spanked, she does show bewilderment and consternation, but her ambivalence is temporary and never reaches the level of conflict which might be uncomfortable to watch. Lee never seems humiliated; this truly painful feeling is present only symbolically, as if the screenwriter used anorexia and cutting to represent emotions she did not understand and was incapable of rendering. Right after spanking her, the Boss hands Lee the letter she has re-typed with the comment "good job;" a look of sweet, simple joy possesses her face. These emotions are not incongruent with S/M. But considering that Lee is supposed to be an inexperienced and emotionally frail person, it is remarkable that she understands this so quickly—remarkably facile. Debby's arousal is so intense it nearly breaks her. Lee's arousal is pleasant and improving, as is Lee herself.

This is not to say that the film shirks ambivalence entirely. It's the boss (played by James Spader) who is confused and anguished here, and it was an interesting choice to make him so. The jerk-off scene is done with a close-up on him, and Spader's face subtly reveals sexual feeling that is deep enough to include sadness and vulnerability as well as furtive, guilty meanness which he does not himself understand. (Not cruelty; meanness. Cruelty is too strong a word for this film.) These qualities, as they are revealed, give him complexity and make you feel for him.

However, his ambiguity comes too dear, at the expense of hers. Gyllenhaal is a delightful and unaffected presence, so genuinely pleasing that she almost redeems a character verging on total insipidity. In one scene, in which she awkwardly spanks herself at home, her face and body are alive, radiating animal determination and geekiness that is funny and touching. It makes one doubly sorry that delightful and pleasing were all that the character was finally allowed to be. But he so emphasizes this perceived beauty that it becomes one-dimensional. As the film progresses, Lee begins to seem like a fantasy madonna in her unconditional approval and affirmation of her conflicted lover. When the boss has a crisis about what they're doing and fires Lee, any unpleasant feelings of hurt and anger on her part are quickly transcended. She's all the more accepting and approving, declaring that she wants to "get to know him" before she glues herself to his desk and starves herself for three days. If only the film had ended there, at the desk, its relentlessly positive fantasy could've been leavened with ambiguity, an open place that allowed the viewer his or her own response. But no; the boss lifts Lee out of the chair and carries her upstairs where a curative bath awaits her. In the next sequence they are wed. The "take-away" here is that S/M here is not only painless, it's therapeutic: it has made both characters more confident, better-looking, happier, freer and self-actualized. Best of all, it has lead them straight to marriage!

The original screenplay, a sort of theoretical S/M romper room, was more real than this; in it, for example, Lee cries the first time she is spanked. But there is none of that in the film, which is like the flag for the S/M section of the gay pride parade reading "We Used to Be Sick, Now We're Safe." One critic praised the film for "opening up avenues of feeling and experience," for illuminating "the dark corners of the psyche." And it does illuminate these dark corners, just as dozens of American movies illuminate them every year—by shining a perfectly happy ending on them, so bright in this case that you can't see anything dark at all. This insistence on the positive may seem compassionate, but it rarely is, for it cannot tolerate anything that is not happy and winning. I first saw *Secretary* at the director's house with several of his friends. During the opening scenes, while Lee elegantly maneuvered in an elaborate bondage costume, a woman loudly burst out: "She's not some helpless little victim! She's IN CONTROL and she's doing JUST FINE!" She spoke as if through clenched teeth, and considering that no one had suggested that Lee *was* a victim, her vehemence was startling. This vehemence, which may be the real driving motor of the film, revolves around what has become a contentious cultural belief: that Americans want to be victims, and that such "victimhood" must be denounced or denied.

But I think that this apparent desire to be a victim cloaks an opposing dread, that Americans are in truth profoundly, neurotically terrified of being victims, ever, in any way. This fear is conceivably one reason we are waging a particularly vicious and gratuitous war—because Americans couldn't tolerate feeling like victims, even briefly. I think it is the reason every boob with a hang-nail has been clogging the courts and haunting talk shows across the land telling his/her "story" and trying to get redress for the last twenty years. Whatever the suffering is, it's not to be endured, for God's sake, not felt and never, ever accepted. It's to be triumphed over. And because some things cannot be triumphed over unless they are first accepted and endured; because indeed, some things cannot be triumphed over at all, the "story" must be told again and again in endless pursuit of a happy ending. To be human is finally to be a loser, for we are all fated to lose our carefully constructed sense of self, our physical strength, our health, our precious dignity and finally our lives. A refusal to tolerate this reality is a refusal to tolerate life, and art based on the empowering message and positive image is just such a refusal.

What *Secretary* the movie and *Secretary* the story have in common is the theme of awakening. In the movie, the heroine awakens to her masochistic sexuality and lives happily ever after. In the story, the heroine awakens to her masochistic sexuality and learns a hard truth: that she is a small, fallible container for primary force beyond her understanding. In the end, her self, that fetish object of anorexics and cutters, has become unknown to her. And it's not "such a bad feeling at all." She is alone on an ocean, with no idea where she's headed, without any nice boss to hold her hand. Whether or not this is a terrible ending is unclear even to me. She may discover uncharted territory or she may be eaten by sharks. But whether or not she learns to negotiate the sea she finds herself cast upon, it will remain unknown to her—as it will remain to all of us.

*

In spite of all this—I understand why people liked the film. In a perfect world, sweet, understanding masochists would meet and marry sweet, understanding sadists and go on to have hot, conflict-free fun in perpetuity. How can I be sarcastic about the earnestness of *Secretary* when, fifteen years ago, I gave an interview to the *Wall Street Journal* in which I earnestly told the world that "masochism is normal"? If falsely positive movies can be made about everybody else, why not make them about sadomasochists, who are surely an under-served population in this regard? Am I too high and mighty to scorn the need for empowerment, always, in every case? Who hasn't, at least once, come out of a movie glad to be uplifted, even if the uplift is specious? Apparently young girls felt empowered by *Pretty Woman*, and I say bless their impressionable hearts. Indeed, somewhere, in a parallel universe, I can imagine my character Debby watching *Secretary* and feeling empowered!

Incidentally, Steven Shainberg was right about *Pretty Woman*. Some years after our initial conversation, I came across the original script titled "Three Thousand." It's a beautiful piece of work, a dark and powerful story about a loser and a victim. And it was ruined by philistines.

2003

Beg For Your Life: On the Films of Laurel Nakadate

I am getting into this by going the long way around.

Once when I was driving in my car, I heard a story by Ira Sher read on the radio. I don't know if I remember it accurately because I was driving and it was a long time ago. It was an amazing story, but still, it was just a story and so for a long time I forgot it. It came back with a lot of force when I saw Laurel Nakadate's 2009 film "Exorcism in January." I am not sure why.

Ira Sher's story is about a bunch of restless kids who live somewhere in a small town in a desert. The narrator's home life is screwed up in some way, I don't recall exactly how, maybe divorce. For fun, he goes with his friends to explore in the desert, and one day they discover something dramatic: a guy trapped at the bottom of a dry well. He pleads with them to get help, and instead, they go home and make up a basket of food with water for him. He is very thankful and asks when help is coming. They are non-committal. This goes on for a few days. The man starts to get desperate. He says "You told your parents, right? Help is coming, right?" They don't really answer. It's not that they don't care. It's more that it's very exciting to have him as their special thing.

*

There is no literal connection between Nakadate's film and Sher's story. "Exorcism in January" is not about kids or abandonment; the film is in a strange way about friendship. In the film, Nakadate plays a girl in a hot pink bra who wakes up in a near-empty room of light, puts on cowboy boots and goes to visit an old guy who lives in a dark, dirty apartment lit like a Dutch masterpiece. She asks him how he is and he says he's pretty down. She asks why and he says it's a chemical imbalance in his brain. Or maybe a demonic possession; maybe an exorcism would help, he says, maybe she could pray over him and shake rattles and drive the spirits away. She asks when he wants to do it and he says tomorrow. She says okay and she leaves; his eyes follow her out. The next day she wakes again in her room of light and puts a pink shirt over her pink bra and puts on her boots. He is lying on his bed in his dark chaotic room. You hear her voice, and it is the voice of a child; she is saying "Go away spirits, go away" and he is repeating her words and shaking his hands while his cat licks itself. "Shake them out," she says. "Lick them out. Bad spirits go away." "I don't want you here," he says, "go away." She kneels by his bed and says "Go away." The next day she wakes again in underwear, in bright light. She goes into his dark apartment and asks if he's better. He says, yes, he is. He thinks the exorcism worked. She says he should give an acceptance speech "about how great it is." He does, sort of.

*

The kids in the story keep bringing the man food and water, but they never tell their parents. They don't tell because they are afraid they will get into trouble for not telling. Eventually he realizes what is going on. Eventually he asks, what are your names?

One of them answers without thinking and the others go "Shhh!" And they go away.

*

The man in the movie is named Larry. He is a friend of Laurel's; he wrote the script for "An Exorcism in January."

*

Laurel Nakadate wrote and directed *The Wolf Knife*, which is about two 16-year-old girls named Chrissy (Christina Kolozs-vary) and June (Julie Potratz) who decide to go to Nashville to find Chrissy's father. The decide to do this after Chrissy's mom tells them there is a rapist in the neighborhood with a gun; immediately after she tells them this, the mom's boyfriend proposes. The boyfriend pulls a diamond ring out of his shirt pocket, the same pocket from which he earlier pulled a pair of underpants which he gave to Chrissy. He says he wants Chrissy's mom to be his princess forever. He keeps saying princess, not queen, even though Chrissy's mom is not young. The girls get up and leave in disgust. Later they lie in twin beds, and Chrissy tells June that she's heard her mom and the boyfriend having sex and that they say gross, aggressive things; the boyfriend says "Beg for your life." June laughs and Chrissy snaps at her. Chrissy decides they should go to Nashville to look for her dad; they flee in the dead of night.

Nakadate does not act in this film but the actress who plays Chrissy is a dead-ringer for how we might imagine Nakadate at 16. (I don't know why this seems to matter but it does.) She is an intensely physical person, this girl, and it's a willful, *intelligent* physicality, like her body came into the world knowing things, not specifically carnal things, but deep, complicated things. Her dark, thick-lashed eyes, though, have the questing, hurt look of

99

someone who *knows*, yet still doesn't quite want to believe what she knows, and is looking to find something less ... well, less insane. It's the expression of someone who's socialized mind isn't prepared for what the rest of her is taking in.

June is less powerfully physical, with more question than knowledge in her limbs. Her eyes are beyond questing, they are yearning, blindly, with no idea what for. Chrissy is clearly the dominant one between them, with far greater will and imagination. What the two have in common, what makes them seem like sisters, is the beautiful way they inhabit the fecund density of adolescence in bloom. Nakadate drenches the viewer in this quality with her close-ups; through the intensity of her gaze, the girls bodily express vital, amoral goodness, good as a plant or animal is good just by being what it is. Done up in wet, shiny lipsticks, heavy eye make-up and tight, neon-colored clothes, the girls radiate, in their skin, lips and eyes, the abiding purity of a primary impulse seeking to find a shape in the bizarrely shaped landscape of twenty-first-century humanity. It's not just the girls. Grass, trees, animals, people—everything in Nakadate's world is burstingly alive and bright with the need to be what it is. There is an almost tragicomical tension between this ferocious, innocent need and the perversity of the human culture/character through which it must come; it is a tension that at some point, and repeatedly, will become anguished.

As it turns out, Chrissy isn't looking for her father. She's going to visit her retired third grade teacher who she says is a really nice guy. When June discovers this she is angry and wants to go back home. But without Chrissy, she is simply not resourceful enough. So they go see Mr. Dews. Nearly an old man now, Mr. Dews is living with his elderly father; he looks a louche ruin, as though years of crushing disappointment have crushed him into the shape of an elegant troll. And yet—within this shape, he still wants and seeks to be. His voice is a nightmare of nuance, full of humor and horror, and with it he croaks at Chrissy as from the bottom of a well. And then he pulls her in. Their dialogue is a masterpiece of misshapen, mixed-up emotion, crashing from tenderness to rapacity to loathing to longing to pity to remnants of real affection and respect which pathetically shimmer—and then are violated all in the tonal changes of the wretched man's voice. The visit ends with Chrissy squashed up against a mirror, confessing something that June did that she wishes she could've done. Her third-grade teacher is devouring what he thinks is her innocent shame and she is feeding it to him. As awful as this is, it may be preferable to what she really feels, for her shame is in being unwanted and hating June for it.

But it is June who cries. She cries and won't say much to Chrissy, who feels guilty and so begins to bully her friend with cruel little gestures, like forcing a straw into her mouth and commanding her to "drink more." June finally fights back—and then the wolf knife comes out. And still the girls' skin and eyes and lips continue to seek, to yearn, to be. As does the earth and grass and sky around them, with heart-breaking amoral goodness.

*

In her 2006 film *Beg for Your Life*, Nakadate is a girl who points guns at old guys and says "Beg for your life!" She does this for laughs; a lot of other stuff happens, old guys kidnap the girl and she kind of makes one of them kill her except she's not dead. Music plays, the last song is about "making love out of nothing at all." But because the film is called "Beg for Your Life," I'm thinking that's the highlight. The girl seems to really like saying it, and the old guys seem to really like it too. One of the men starts cracking up in the middle of it, and how could he not, it's ridiculous funny, weird sweet and also a little bit horrible. These old guys aren't actors professionally. They are old guys she met in places like the Home Depot parking lot, who came up and talked to her because she's pretty. Some of them are mentally ill. Many of them, like Larry, she came to know well.

*

I never got to hear the end of Ira Sher's story because I had to get out of the car. The last part I did hear—the narrative had shifted away from the man in the well to the protagonist's problematic home life. So I don't know what happened. My guess is that they left him down there. Maybe at the end the narrator went back and shouted down and got no answer. But I don't know. It was a great story anyway.

*

Someone I know who saw "The Wolf Knife" before I did described it as being about "girls making bad choices." Which is true. Except that in the world of "The Wolf Knife," there really don't seem to be good choices. In the world of "The Wolf Knife" there are swimming pools full of lapping light and soft plapping sounds; there are peacocks and flowers and bright blue lawn chairs and unless you are perfect you will need an ass lift when you are 26; your sweating blank-eyed mother dances joylessly in the attic and her boyfriend pulls panties from his pocket. There is ice cream and giant wooden pictures of water and sky; white prisoners are more glamorous than black prisoners and the cute guy you like only wants a hand-job from you and then you never talk again, but the other cute guy fucks your friend and she doesn't even tell you; the light turns your friend's skin orange and yellow and you are orange and yellow too, and her eyes are all occluded. You make her lie on her back on a dinosaur statue in public so her crotch bone sticks out and take her picture. Mr. Dews says, "Legs and

102

hips and shoulders and eyes and lips and ankles and hair and eyebrows and nose" in the dirtiest voice you ever heard and you can see what he means even though he is talking about you. Your mother's engagement ring comes out your mouth. Somebody is down in a hole and people know and no one knows. Sometimes you think you know who it is; sometimes it is someone else. Sometimes it is you. It is horrible. And it is amazing.

2013

The Easiest Thing to Forget: On Carl Wilson's *Let's Talk About Love*

When I first picked up Carl Wilson's *Let's Talk About Love: A Journey to the End of Taste*, I didn't know what Celine Dion sounded like—and I did not live, during 1996–97 in a "Unabomber-like retreat from audible civilization," which Wilson claims is the only circumstance under which one could lack this awful (according to him) knowledge. I started reading anyway because I wondered why someone would write a whole book exploring and trying to reconcile with a singer whose music he hated. I kept reading because I liked Wilson's supple and subtle voice, and because I was increasingly fascinated to see just how much emotion and energy he and apparently hoards of others have expended in hating and despising a singer I had never even noticed.

It's not that I don't know from weird singer-hate: Billy Joel, the early Boy George and Mark McGrath of Sugar Ray all have voices that used to make me inwardly spasm with misanthropic disgust for a few seconds at least. But apparently Celine-haters don't spasm in silence or for seconds, they scream and froth at the mouth *at length*: "... the most wholly repellent woman ever to sing songs of love," spewed Cintra Wilson. "I think most people would rather be processed through the digestive tract of an anaconda than be Celine Dion for a day." Bitch, excuse me? We're not talking about Bernie Madoff or the Abu Graib torture team, this is a pop singer who annoys Your Excellency. In response to the relentless snideness described by Wilson about Dion's teeth, her Quebecois accent, her kooky arm-movements, her clueless fans (whom some asshole in the UK sneeringly imagined as "overweight children" and "Grannies"), by page 18, I was solidly in Dion's corner without hearing a note; I figured that anyone who got so many pricks so agitated had to be doing something right.

Then came page 23, on which Wilson informs the reader that the most "widely mocked minutes of Celine Dion's career" occurred when she had the vulgarity to get all emotional about the victims of Hurricane Katrina on Larry King, crying even, and doing that arm-movement thing like some kind of spaz; the next day it apparently went viral under headings like "Celine Dion Goes Crazy!" For me anyway, that's when the book became about something more than Celine Dion, pop music or tastes. Wilson skillfully uses the Larry King incident to segue at graceful length into a description of Dion's Quebecois cultural roots which, he says, explain why she "fails most non-fans' authenticity tests" and why "her personal touchstones are off the map," this being true because Quebec's idiosyncratic pop culture and Francophone sense of oppression are "a null set in the popular imagination." Wilson can show, with his lengthy analysis, why Dion's passionate defense of poor New Orleanians who "looted" busted-up stores was as "culturally sound" as Kanye West's speech the following week, and he's very interesting while doing it; Dion's personal and cultural background makes a good read. But. While there have always been and always will be stunted creatures who make fun of people for showing emotion that said creatures are uncomfortable with, why does a plainly sophisticated, generous and intelligent critic need to marshal lengthy cultural analysis to explain to his equally sophisticated cohort why a person might get emotional and even cry at the sight of her fellows wretchedly suffering day after day? Really, you have to explain why that is "culturally sound"?

I didn't ask these questions the first time I read the book because I got so involved in Wilson's parsing of the "signifiers," "referents" and "touchstones" that make up the horrible baroque language of modern criticism, a layering upon layering of assumptions, interpretations and second-guesses trip-wired to catch the uncool. The importance of cool in this culture is something that Wilson spends a great deal of time on, and is depressingly convincing about:

> The virtuosity that cool audiences today applaud, the sort Celine always fumbles, is not about having a multioctave voice or flamenco-fast fingers: it's about being able to manipulate signs and symbols, to hitch them up and decouple them in a blink of an eye, to quote Homer but in the voice of Homer Simpson. It's the kind of virtuosity an advertiser deploys to hook multiple demographics, as well as the playful or caviling way of the postmodern artist.

What Wilson is describing, in this section and throughout the book, is a world of illusory shared experiences, ready-made identities, manipulation and masks so dense and omnipresent that in this world, an actual human face is ludicrous or "crazy;" a world in which authenticity is jealously held sacrosanct and yet is often unwelcome or simply unrecognizable when it appears.

Wilson eventually seeks out and gets to know some Celine Dion fans, one of whom is Sophoan, a young Christian Cambodian-American who spent his first five years in a refugee camp on the border of Cambodia and Thailand. Wilson maintains his equilibrium as Sophoan describes his love for Celine Dion, but loses it when Sophoan reveals that, as a toddler interned in a camp with a dirt floor, he really loved Phil Collins, especially the song "Groovy Kind of Love": "What on earth," muses Wilson, "does [Collins'] goopiest tune ... sound like to a displaced Cambodian five-year-old? (I suppose not knowing the word 'groovy' would help.)"

I *think* the parenthetical is meant to be funny but still, on reading the question, I almost answered it out loud: "Gentle, Carl. To *any* toddler the song would sound comforting and gentle. To a toddler surrounded by anxiety, fear, sadness and loss, that sound would be especially nurturing, *especially* the sound 'groovy,' with its delicious 'ooo' and fun 'eee.'" (These same sounds are also nurturing to adults forced to live with chronic fear, sadness and loss, which is probably why Dion and singers like her are (according to Wilson) popular in Iraq and Afganistan.) At this point in the book, I had come to like and admire Wilson for his empathic and imaginative willingness to pick his way through the dark maze of signifiers and referents in order to see past his own received ideas. Still, I wanted to say, Good grief man, music is about *sound*; that social meaning shit is ... basically shit. Fun, interesting shit, maybe, but ...

Speaking of sound, either mid-book or on finishing, I finally listened to Celine Dion on YouTube. I heard three songs, including the *Titanic* one. I thought her voice was pretty, even beautiful at moments, but her overall sound made little impression; I probably *had* heard her and forgotten it. Her appearance on Larry King however did make an impression; it struck me as absolutely sincere and sane. That thousands would actually spend time watching this interview so they could jeer at it, jeering especially that Dion (a singer!) had the nerve to sing a song after her speech, seemed not merely cynical but neurotically detached from reality: Dion's response wasn't only moral, it showed a sort of biologically-based empathy that understands the physical vulnerability of humans in the world. Newsflash: real humans are connected with each other whether they like it or not. They are awkward and dumb and wave their arms around if they get upset enough; real humans *all* have personal touchstones that are "off the map" because *there is no map*. We are so maplessly, ridiculously uncool that whole cultures and subcultures, whole personalities even, have been built to hide our ridiculousness from ourselves. These structures are sometimes very elegant and a lot of fun and fun to talk about too. But our ridiculous vulnerability is perhaps the most authentic thing about us, and we scorn it at our peril—yet scorn it we do.

At the end of *Let's Talk About Love*, Wilson concludes that Celine Dion will remain "securely uncool" and that this gives him "the heart to go on." I *think* this means that he's realized that someone he had despised for reasons having nothing to do with her is just a person making art that he can like or dislike, but that his likes or dislikes don't reflect on the fundamental quality of her humanity or his, a quality which independently exists and will "go on" outside of any systematized set of social/artistic judgments.

It seems the most obvious thing in the world. But in the middle of writing this reaction to Carl Wilson's reaction to Celine Dion, something funny happened: I went to see a reading by a writer who had been described to me as great, and I not only failed to find him great, I found him bad, obnoxiously bad, bad to the point that I was a-boil in my chair as I listened to him hold forth. When he was done I turned to the person next to me and said "What an idiot." That night I called someone and expanded on that "thought," using words like "buffoon," and "conceited pig." I don't know how long I went on about it, but it was *much longer than seconds*. It wasn't until I hung up that I heard my own words in my head: *Bitch, excuse me?*

This seems to me the real substance of Wilson's book, and why it is more than an intelligent discourse on a small, specialized segment of society: the most obvious thing in the world is the easiest thing to forget, especially regarding any subject that you care about, *especially* when that subject is an art form full of costumed personalities making their most private experience into publicly projected stories, where real and unreal are fantastically or oafishly mixed. In this non-stop torrent of personae, audience and performers both, Carl Wilson has slowly and patiently come to find and respect one human soul regardless of his cherished "likes;" it's a beautiful reminder to see someone do that in any context.

2013

Icon: On Linda Lovelace

Icon of freedom and innocent carnality; icon of brokenness and confusion; icon of a wound turned into or disguised as pleasure-source; icon of sexual victimization, sexual power, irreconcilable oppositions; icon of 1970s America; icon of Every-woman. And just another skinny white girl with average looks and a little flat voice, a type you barely notice even if some version of her is everywhere.

I saw Linda Lovelace* in *Deep Throat* because my boyfriend was the projectionist at a hippie film co-op. It was 1972 and I was 17; my boyfriend was 25 and neither of us was interested in porn, which we thought of as a corny old person thing. But *Deep Throat,* an X-Rated comedy about a woman whose clitoris is in her throat, was supposed to be something different, and we were curious, then won over by the film's dirty goof-ballery. "She just seemed to like it so much," said my boyfriend, and his voice was not salacious as much as tickled. I liked the movie too, it was funny—but *liking* and arousal are very different. I wasn't excited

---

*I am not using the surname "Borman" because it is the public persona "Linda Lovelace" that this essay is most concerned with.

by *Deep Throat*, and the only thing I could really remember about it afterward was Lovelace's sweet smile and the strange expression in her eyes, a look that I could not define and still can't, a look which was not happy yet which seemed to go with her smile.

I was however wildly excited by the next movie I saw at the co-op, a film that on the face of it has nothing in common with *Deep Throat*, but which remains, in my imagination, weirdly linked with the porn comedy: it was Carl Dreyer's *The Passion of Joan of Arc*, an emotionally stunning silent film made in 1928 about the persecution, psychological torture and death of an inexplicably, helplessly powerful 19-year-old girl. I'm sure it sounds ridiculously arty, but trust me, my reaction was not artistic. I was horrified by this film, but also moved and so aroused that I was embarrassed to be in public, even in the dark. I don't *like* images of persecution or death or torture, but liking was irrelevant; *Passion* demanded a powerful response and my body gave it.

Anyway, in 1980, when Linda Lovelace wrote a book (with journalist Mike McGrady) about her experience called *Ordeal*, then joined Catherine McKinnon's anti-porn movement, I fleetingly remembered her sweet, strange-eyed smile, and how different it seemed from the woman claiming that anyone who watched *Deep Throat* was watching her being raped. I was vaguely sad but not that surprised; it seemed just one more piece of senseless effluvia flying past.

Fast forward to 2012, when not one but two mainstream biopics about Linda Lovelace were being made at the same time; I learned of these films because of a brief involvement with a guy who had some vague connection with one of the films as well as very strong opinions on its subject. He felt nothing but contempt for Lovelace, whom he described as a deeply stupid liar who refused to take responsibility for any of her actions, including her participation in pre-*Throat* porn loops, particularly one in which she enthusiastically received a dog. He told me that in *Ordeal* she claimed, among other things, that she was forced by her husband/ pimp, Chuck Traynor,* to "do" the dog, but that "everyone" knew it was a lie, that she was "into it," that is, she liked it.

This was all news to me, but I shrugged and said, I don't blame her. We've all done things which, while not embarrassing at the time, *would* be embarrassing if projected on a public movie screen. Besides she had kids; if you had kids, would you want to talk about dog-fucking with them? But, my friend said, then she turned on Women Against Pornography and said *they* used her too. I said, they probably did, those women are bonkers. He came back, but *then* she posed for a magazine called *Leg Show*, to which I said, so what, that's not really porn and she probably needed the money. We changed the subject and broke up that night.

But the conversation made me care about Linda Lovelace in a way I previously had not, and made me want to defend her. It also made me curious; she and her husband/pimp Chuck Traynor are dead (both in 2002), as is *Deep Throat* director Gerry Damiano and Lovelace's co-star Harry Reems, so why was a grown man talking like a school-yard bully about her ten years later? Why was her story suddenly of such pop-cultural interest that, forty-plus years after *Deep Throat*, two mainstream film companies wanted to tell it?

When the biopic titled *Lovelace* came out the following year (the other, *Inferno*, floundered and was killed), I saw it and became something more than curious. *Lovelace* is a candy-colored feel-good story of a nice girl forced into porn by an abusive husband, who nonetheless blooms with the attention of celebrities like Hugh Hefner, is redeemed by feminism, accepted by her family, gets married and starts a family of her own. Critics and viewers

---

*Pronounced "trainer," a name that, in some linguistically-based universe, should've been enough all by itself to get him hauled in on suspicion of *something*.

responded tepidly, but to me the bowdlerization was even more obnoxious than my former friend's contempt. Why, after more than forty years, were people so insistently sanitizing and simplifying this story?

I shouldn't have wondered; *Deep Throat* was an extreme phenomenon which, whimsically and unselfconsciously, both confirmed and challenged the status quo of masculine privilege by creating a fantasy world of blowjobs that gave pride of place to female orgasm. This preposterous polarity was heightened by the film's combination of high and low (in terms of register or pitch), the way it put together silliness and lightness of spirit with the florid id-imagery of porn, especially the image of its star, an appealing girl happily splitting her pretty face to get huge, hairy dick impossibly far down her throat. Made in six days for $45,500, with sit-com dialogue and a kooky soundtrack, the film grossed $50 million; *Screw*'s Al Goldstein fell in love, the mafia made a killing (literally), President Nixon condemned it, New York Mayor Lindsay banned it, and the glitterati lined up to see it, including Jack Nicholson, Truman Capote, Liz Taylor and Jackie O. Harry Reems was arrested and eventually did time for obscenity; Linda Lovelace became an international celebrity.

She may've been average-looking, but (in addition to her famous erotic "trick" and her ardent way with it) Lovelace projected the perverse charm of innocence soiled, but blithely so, a fragile, playful persona that was uniquely, darkly radiant, dirty and ethereal both. She appeared at a time that is hard to imagine now, when porn has become normalized and commodified to the point that middle-class teenagers might sport license plates that read PORN STAR and actual porn stars are featured on mainstream news websites; 1972 was a transitional time, both libertine and innocent in every direction, with traditional values asserted as aggressively as they were rebelled against. It was a time when many people must've found it wonderful to see a sweet-faced

young woman with a touchingly delicate figure and a girly voice
swallowing throbbin' gristle till her nose ran, yet whom you could
watch without feeling nasty *because she liked it so much.* The 2005
documentary *Inside Deep Throat* includes footage of a press conference at which Lovelace appears in a long pale gown with a
rose in her teeth; she looks anything but average, she is beautiful,
puckishly so, and she is surrounded by absolutely gaga men who
look as if they are witnessing the arrival of a woman riding in
from another world astride a thunderbolt, a world in which good
and evil cum together with joy, and *anything* is allowed without
consequence.

It is poignant to consider this explosion of glamor and sexual
exuberance emanating from an utterly unglamorous, small,
abused and abusing couple, but—for a minute it seemed like anything *was* allowed, and when anything is allowed, what really *is*
abuse?

Abused or not, Lovelace suddenly had offers she never dreamed
of, from television, movies and lecture circuits, and she gamely
tried to make use of it all, trollish husband in tow. But either
because she lacked the talent or because she was simply too
overwhelmed by the whole thing, none of it worked for her; she
dropped out of sight, divorcing Chuck and marrying childhood
friend Larry Marchiano. Until, that is, she produced *Ordeal* and
re-emerged as an anti-porn activist. Her besotted fans were disappointed; her former colleagues were *angry,* and in some cases
hurt—according to porn star Annie Sprinkle, *Deep Throat's* director was "heart-broken" by her claims.

The Other Hollywood, by Legs McNeil and Jennifer Osborne
(with Peter Pavia), is an "Uncensored Oral History of the Porn
Industry," and it is jammed with people expressing their anger
and disgust at Lovelace—even people who plainly state that yes,
Chuck Traynor beat his wife. "I mean, this was a woman who
never took responsibility for her own shitty choices—but instead

114

blamed everything that happened in her life on porn. You know, 'The devil made me do it.'" In a personal exchange with me, Annie Sprinkle was gentler about it: "I do think Linda was in an abusive relationship. And she was definitely traumatized by it ... And I strongly believe that she had a ball doing *Deep Throat* and that she was treated like a star, and went through a horrible time simultaneously with her husband ... I'm sure she also associated *Deep Throat* with that horrible time in her life."

I liked that interpretation and took it further, possibly in a too-romantic direction. I thought that the relationship must've at least started as consensual, that there was probably an element of coersion from Chuck that was part fear and part willing excitement, but that at some point the excitement tipped over into real fear, and that eventually Lovelace could not tell where one ended and the other began. I wondered if Traynor, pimp that he was, knew for sure. Once out of the relationship, I imagined that Lovelace simply lacked the confidence to describe what she did and felt in a nuanced way, and that the thing was very, very nuanced and contradictory. So she went with either "I liked it" or "I was raped."

This is a very rational, mild and forgiving way to think of an experience that was none of the above. Just how "none of the above" it might've been became apparent when I read *Ordeal*. That book, which is now out of print, has been so dismissed that I almost didn't read it. I can see why it was dismissed; the experience it describes is so relentlessly, ridiculously miserable, so helpless and hapless, so utterly incongruous with how Lovelace initially presented herself. Some of it does strain credulity; as I read the beginning of it, I asked myself out loud "Where were her instincts?" It's a good question: if her portrayal of Chuck Traynor is at all accurate, he was the kind of guy that even a very young and naïve girl could see coming from a mile off; you don't need special shrewdness or even much experience to recognize a predator, all you need is a working animal instinct. But some people's instincts have been ruined. Some people's instincts have been so ruined by such disrespectful treatment that, for them, disrespect is not merely a norm, it has a kind of hyper-reality that is absolutely compelling. Such people don't necessarily identify as masochistic in a conscious way. They are sometimes just apparently weird people whose strange ways of dealing with the world can make them a pain in the ass. It's hard to want to know them—that is, to know how hurt they are, and how intractable the damage is. I'm not sure I believe everything in *Ordeal*, but even if half of it is true, expressions like "nuanced and contradictory" or "having a ball" and " being treated like a star" seem woefully off the mark.

But, while it expresses a low opinion of porn, *Ordeal* doesn't actually blame porn for anything. The book is appreciative of some people in the business (for example the late porn star Andrea True) and depicts *Deep Throat* as a big step up from the stuff Lovelace says she was forced into previously. She describes Gerry Damiano and most of the other people involved with the film as relatively decent and considerate, including a sound man who offered to protect her from Traynor if she gave him a "signal." As grotesque as it is, I can't dismiss it; too much of it rings true. But it's also impossible to dismiss the appealing, even delightful way she looks in *Deep Throat*, or her other-worldly radiance in the following press conference and interviews. In spite of her eerie, sometimes dead-looking eyes, there is nothing in her voice or body language that suggests terror or victimization, not even during a scene in which she's pretending to be menaced by a pretend rapist with a gun. Really, she *does* look like she's having a ball. A ball in hell maybe, but a ball nonetheless.

This equal-and-opposite mixed signage is what makes Lovelace into a compelling, even profound figure, a lost soul and powerful icon, defiled innocent and sexual rock star who posed for a skin mag at fifty-two. All these years later, her redemption is important for feminists (and not only those with an anti-porn fixation) because, in spite of her Sadeian trajectory, her experience is a fun-house version of the sometimes excruciating contradictions that many women experience in relation to sex.

Consider this mild and typical anecdote: a friend of mine, now in her 50s, told me how, in her 20s, that every time she would walk into her neighborhood bar in NYC's East Village, this same guy would grab her breasts and everybody would laugh; she said thinking about it now made her furious. When I asked her what she did at the time, she said she laughed too because she didn't know what else to do. And I remember what she was like in her 20s; she flirted and giggled a lot, and she loved attention. So which is true, the giggly girl who just laughed when the guy grabbed her, or the angry woman in her 50s? Now consider this more extreme contradiction: a therapist once told me that some women orgasm when they are raped. I had never heard this before and found it hard to believe. I said, "So, if the rapist said 'she liked it,' he would be telling the truth." The therapist said, no, she did not like it. But for some people the adrenal arousal of terror turns into global arousal that becomes sexual.

I thought of that when I read in *The Other Hollywood* that Linda was constantly turned on, that she was "soaking wet," and that she really seemed to be "into it" with the dog. In *Ordeal*, Lovelace writes that she was forced into the scene with the dog, that there was actually a gun on the set. But in *The Other Hollywood*, actress Sharon Mitchell says that when she briefly walked onto the set it "didn't look like they were forcing her to do anything," rather that it "looked like they were forcing the dogs!" Mitchell says that she was so upset by the sight of Linda's arousal that she became terrified and ran down the stairs. The first striking thing about this anecdote is Mitchell's mean-girl brutality; did she realize how many people would talk with the same contempt about her? Was the sight of arousal really so terrifying? Or was she running from terror itself, terror blended with arousal so completely that she didn't consciously know what she was looking at or running from? The second striking thing is that although everyone else involved describes one dog on the set, Mitchell apparently saw "dogs"—kind of like Lovelace seeing a gun that everyone else says wasn't there. Chuck Traynor did hit Linda and he did own guns. If he ever pointed a gun at Linda, even once, in her mind it was probably always there.

Or not. Maybe there was no gun and she knew it. Maybe she was terrified anyway. Fear is powerful sometimes even when there is no immediate threat. Sometimes it motivates people without their knowing it except in hindsight, if at all.

When I was 17 I was violently raped. It was horrible, but I got through it and did not believe it affected me over-much. It did not inhibit me sexually; in the years following the experience I was promiscuous, even aggressively so. Sometimes I had sex without really knowing why (by which I mean I did it when I wasn't really interested), but that seemed true of many, many people at the time. Then one day when I was 19 something happened. I was with a guy and we were fooling around on my bed, still fully clothed. Playfully, he raised himself over me, grabbed my wrists and pinned them. I went completely blank. I don't know how else to describe it. As he put it later, my body went limp and my eyes "empty." Scared himself, he let go of me and said something like "What's wrong?" I said "I thought you were going to start hitting me." Clearly taken aback, he replied "I would never do that, how could you think that?" I said "I don't know," and I meant it; I had no idea how much fear I'd been carrying and was so surprised by my own blanking out that I didn't even understand it at first. We talked some—I don't remember if I told him about being raped or not—but sex was out of the question.

That incident made me realize that I was sometimes having sex because I was afraid that if I didn't I would be raped or hit, even when the men in question did not threaten me in any way. This was not always the case, I had natural feelings. But sometimes fear motivated me without my being aware of it until that one boy's gesture brought it out of hiding. Even then it was so *physically* present in me that I couldn't stop having sex I didn't fully want for almost two years after I realized what was going on.

Because of experiences like this—not just mine, but those which other women have described to me—it's hard for me to see the Lovelace story as a simple matter of her lying or not. Even if there was no gun and Lovelace knew it I can't see that kind of lie as coming from one simple motivation. Maybe Lovelace enjoyed what she did to the point of wallowing in it, including the abuse that came with it, and then years later, when she was ravaged, angry and broke, rewrote it and came to believe the revision. Maybe she started out liking it and came to hate it or liked it sometimes and hated it other times. Maybe she never *liked* it, but was masochistically *aroused* by it; maybe she hated it straight-up but did it anyway. Not many people could describe experiencing any of this accurately let alone honestly, especially if it was *all* true. That is, if she felt all of the above in some hellish combination, and was so torn by the opposition that she developed a fragmented public self, one which smiled and was delightful when prompted or which assumed an anti-porn stance when prompted, with nothing fully developed in support of either.

This last, terrible idea makes me remember my stunned blankness of so long ago, blankness that I acted out of for years and which, frankly, was not exclusively about rape. Blankness is a kind of dead zone, and action that comes from blankness happens in fragments. I know what it's like to be pulled in too many directions to make sense of, but to want to live and to engage so much that you act regardless. It's a hard way to be, but at least I had the space and time to try and understand my experience as best I could. Lovelace didn't have that ordinary luxury because of her

fame. Becoming famous for being yourself is now an American fixation; Linda Lovelace lived the dream, and how. But what would
it be like to be famous for being yourself if you didn't know what
your "self" was? Imagine projecting and being projected into the
world, on a massive scale, as someone who has no complex emotions, who is all persona, in this case a persona that is all about
having one particular kind of sex with whoever. Because people
liked the persona, it must've felt good at first, hell, it must've felt
great. But some of the worst things in the world feel that way. At
first.

In the documentary *The Real Linda Lovelace* Chuck Traynor
described his wife this way: "Everything she did, she had to be
told how to do it and when to do it and why she was doing it
... you always had to tell her what to do." This is self-serving;
it's possibly true. After Traynor and Lovelace split, he married
Marilyn Chambers, and by most accounts the relationship was
good for the eleven years that it lasted. Eric Danville, a friend and
fan of Lovelace (and author of *The Complete Linda Lovelace*), once
asked Chambers if she ever met Linda; she said no, but that she
once overheard her screaming at Chuck on the phone while he
winced and held the receiver away from his ear. In an interview
she gave before her death in 2009*, Chambers was asked what it
was like to be married to "the infamous Chuck Traynor" and she
defended him all the way, characterizing Lovelace's book as "75%
BS" and Chuck as "an average Joe Blow kind of guy" who knew
what "turned on the average guy." According to a 2013 article by
Christine Pelisek in *The Daily Beast*, Chambers acknowledged that
Traynor did hit her once but that she "hit him back really hard,"
breaking two fingernails; she said that Linda's problem was that
she was "meek." The same *Beast* article reports that when Chambers and Traynor divorced, she gave him all of her money, that

---

*See girlsandcorpses.com

she died with nothing. That Chambers accepted the rules of the pimp's game, and played by them till the very end, even to her disadvantage, suggests a kind of gallantry or integrity that might, in another time and context, be referred to as "being a lady." I admire it. But I don't understand why she needed to disparage Lovelace for being "meek" or (it seems to me) for not really knowing that there was a game being played, let alone what the rules were.*

*

That I saw *The Passion of Joan of Arc* in such close proximity to *Deep Throat* is strictly random. Still I am haunted by it. Lovelace was as apparently hapless as St. Joan was fanatically determined, seemingly as ordinary as St. Joan was extraordinary. Yet, in the same way Joan of Arc embodied social and spiritual forces that were most likely beyond her personality, Lovelace was fated to embody extreme and opposing social and sexual forces much too big for the limits of her self, for any self. Both women were torn apart by that which they embodied, yet for a moment glowed with enormous symbolic power. This is what seems the most painful thing about the Lovelace story, more painful even than domestic abuse, to live as a public vector for oppositions that are still too much for this culture, possibly *any* culture to countenance, to burn with the strength of those forces without fully being able to understand or effectively wield them.

In the end Lovelace divorced Marchiano, claiming that he too abused her. She was poor and sick with hepatitis, and, having fallen out with the anti-porn movement, was appearing at porn

---

*A circumstance I find poignant and slightly eerie: Lovelace died on April 22, which was Chamber's birthday; Chuck Traynor died of a heart attack on July 22 exactly three months later.

memorabilia conventions to sign DVD copies of *Deep Throat* and copies of *Ordeal*. The recent film doesn't touch any of this, perhaps because the film-makers felt that in omitting these aspects of the story they were casting their subject in a positive and more sympathetic light, making it easier for the audience to like her. But the bowdlerization does Lovelace a great disservice. As much as anything, her story was about enormous loneliness, and survival against odds that few people could understand; this universal condition makes her moving beyond any specifics of feminism or porn and defies a happy ending.

During *Passion*, one of the twisted inquisitors asks Joan if St. Michael actually spoke to her; as the critic Roger Ebert described it, her face "seems to suggest that whatever happened between Michael and herself was so beyond the scope of the question that no answer is conceivable." The question of whether or not Linda Lovelace was a liar or a victim might be a joke in comparison— but still, I think that whatever happened in that place and time in her life is beyond the scope of the question.

2013

Reading

Mechanical Rabbit: A Review of *Licks of Love* by John Updike

Three years ago, David Foster Wallace wrote a review of John Updike's novel *Toward the End of Time* in which he expressed the opinion that the aging author, along with other "G.M.N.s" (Great Male Narcissists), is a solipsist concerned only with himself and his personal problems. According to Wallace, every character Updike creates is really himself, even when they are not; they are never redeemed by belonging to any "larger unit or community or cause"—yes, they have families, but they don't love them, at least not enough, so that doesn't count. (Nor apparently do jobs and churches count, even though they are the only type of "larger unit" most people belong to.) Having attributed the failings of Updike's characters to their author, Wallace then censoriously extended those failings to an entire generation, deploring the "joyless and anomic self-indulgence of the Me Generation," supposedly epitomized by said author.

This is a perennially popular line of thought, and, on the face of it, a legitimate one: narcissism is bad, communities are good, the novel should have a "broad social sweep." Except that it ignores the following: Even though art is expressed through an individual personality, if it is any good at all it is not about that personality in a literal sense. John Updike does typically feature male protagonists who are selfish, horny, socially conservative, and *irresistible* to young pussy. I'm sure that this reflects Updike's personality in some way, but I would not be so quick to say exactly how, even if Piet, Rabbit, et al. seem to function as mouthpieces for their author's opinions. Because, at his best, Updike places these predictable characters in landscapes as mundane as, yet infinitely more mysterious than, the personalities of those characters seem to be. This is from *Rabbit Redux,* a description of Rabbit and his dad having a talk in the local bar:

> The bar television is running, with the sound turned off. For the twentieth time that day the rocket blasts off, the numbers pouring backwards in tenths of seconds faster than the eye until zero is reached; then the white boiling beneath the tall kettle, the lifting so slow it seems certain to tip, the swift diminishment into a retreating speck, a jiggling star. The men dark along the bar murmur among themselves. They have not been lifted, they are left here. Harry's father mutters at him, prying. "Has she seemed any different to you lately, Harry?"

It's as if Updike has entered a tiny window marked "Rabbit," and, by some inverse law, passed into a universe of energies both light and dark, expanded and contracted, infinite and workaday. In this place, Rabbit's flaws and opinions are just another bit of mutable energy, familiar and yet unknowable as the "jiggling star." If "Rabbit" is how Updike gets to this numinous place, it seems small to stand there fuming that the entry point is not the right one, or worrying that Updike's use of this entry means that he, personally, is narcissistic.

It was with this readiness to defend and adulate that I approached *Licks of Love,* Updike's new, ridiculously titled collection of stories plus a novella. Imagine my distress at finding myself unable to do either. The book isn't bad—it has some lovely moments—but it is nowhere near as good as Updike can be. In some ways, it reads as if he's been listening to his critics and trying to please them. The novella, *Rabbit Remembered*, features Rabbit Angstrom's son Nelson, a mild-mannered, liberal social worker who describes his father as "a narcissist." There are no sex scenes, no distasteful thoughts about "cunts," and the only sexist, racist characters seem meant to be disliked. (There is one exception, when Nelson thinks: "Women lie the way blacks lie. If you're a slave race telling the truth gets you very little." Which strikes me as more weird than offensive; this nerd is walking around imagining himself as a master among slaves?) Generally, the son is kinder, gentler, and far less convincing or compelling than the father.

The same can be said of most of the twelve stories. They revisit the Updikean concerns of family life, adultery, and social drift, and while they are sometimes touching, too often they feel rote and careless. Updike's language can still be sensitive, even beautiful. But too frequently it becomes bloated and grossly imprecise:

> Divorce, which had been flickering at our edges for a decade while our vast pool of children slowly bubbled up through the school grades toward, we hoped, psycho-logical sturdiness, was still rare, and sat raw on Frank, like the red cheek he had been pressing against my wife's as if against a sweaty pillow.

There are exceptions, notably "My Father on the Verge of Disgrace" (a kid discovers his father's petty theft) and "Metamorphosis" (an aging playboy in love with this Korean-American eye doctor persuades her to give him Asian eyelids). All of these are elegant and engaging—but even they lack the surprising changes of depth, the multilevel richness that characterizes Updike's best stories. ("My Father" comes the closest, with its tender, intelligent observations, especially of a high school play in which the dad, to his son's horror, kisses another man for laughs.)

The novella is the most compelling piece in the book, dramatic in the unabashed, sweaty style of a good soap opera. It begins as Rabbit's thirty-nine-year-old illegitimate daughter (Annabelle) comes to visit his widow (Janice), whose current husband (Ronnie) also had sex with Annabelle's mom (Ruth), a some-time prostitute. (Rabbit once had an affair with Ronnie's former wife, Thelma, but never mind.) Annabelle's mother had revealed her father's identity just before dying, and Annabelle's appearance is an unwelcome surprise to everyone but Rabbit's son, Nelson. Nelson's marriage has fallen apart, and he lives a discontented half-life with his mother and stepfather: he's drawn to Annabelle out of a muddled longing for his father. It's as ridiculous as life, and features dialogue like: "I for*bid* anybody getting in touch with this twat." "Ronnie ... this twat may be my *sis*ter."

Even when the dialogue is salty, the effect is often stiff, talking-head-like. Updike's characters have always veered toward the topical, but in the previous Rabbit books, the banal (and realistic) talk was inter-cut with what Anthony Burgess characterized as "the poetry of digression"—that is, apparently unrelated descriptions of, say, a television broadcast in a crummy bar. These digressions are like hidden pockets of thought and feeling, and they subtly elucidate the characters in ways that dialogue alone can rarely achieve. Such poetry is sorely missed here; Updike still uses description and physical detail, but his intuition is off, and so the technique does not serve to deepen or illuminate his scenes.

The book has another problem, one which negatively echoes one of Updike's strengths—his compassion. In the past, the blunt, helpless ugliness of his characters was presented in such a way that you could not overlook it—nor could you overlook how it made them human. The detailed precision with which he drew their lives was never merely aesthetic; it served to locate the reader in the character's skin in a way that went beyond ideology, beyond personal affinity, even beyond words. Whether you liked Rabbit or not, you felt him. You felt his uncertain animal quest-ing in the sensate prose. For Updike to weave such vulnerable animality together with the opinionated stridency of Rabbit or one of his antagonists required a profound, tough-minded com-passion that did not morally let Rabbit, the reader, or the author off the hook. In *Licks of Love*, that compassion has devolved into a lax acceptance that is merely sentimental. Here is Rabbit's widow thinking about their emotionally distant, adultery-ridden mar-riage. "Looking back from this distance, she can't think any more that Harry was all to blame for their early troubles, he had been just trying life on too: life and sex and making babies and finding out who you are."

It is true that time can make even crabby old women forgive that which once seemed unforgivable. But tonally, this passage reminds me of a crowd-pleasing lounge singer who ends his heart-break ballad with cheesy, uplifting chords, his arms open wide, and a brave, desolate twinkle in his eye. Another example from the novella: during Thanksgiving, the oafish Ronnie viciously insults Annabelle's dead mother, calling her a whore who would "fuck anybody;" Annabelle weeps, and Nelson, though he does nothing in the moment, moves out. But the conflict is easily resolved when Janice makes Ronnie call Nelson at work to deliver a grudging apology, during which he refers to Annabelle as a "slick little twat." Then, Nelson feels "right with Ron," and, by New Year's Eve, they're all together again, with Ron smooching the little twat's kisser. [Insert happy music here!]

The same refrain sounds in the stories: in the title piece, a banjo player chosen to take part in a cultural exchange program meets a "little black-haired coffee-fetcher" who says to him, "Sir, you are my God." You know what that means—pretty soon, they're drunk-enly rolling around in her bed. It's not a satisfying experience, but the coffee-fetcher nonetheless becomes obsessed, badgering the banjo player from one end of the Soviet Union to the other with demented love letters. That such extreme emotions have become roused by such a brief encounter is a psychologically rich trope— or at least it ought to be. I imagine it is a strange experience to sleep once with someone who thinks you are a god, to discover that she is profoundly disturbed, and then to be hounded by her across a continent and finally into your own home. I was very interested to see what Updike's character would think and feel about it, as well as what he might imagine the girl to be thinking and feeling. But all he feels is superficial irritation, combined with worry that it will be embarrassing if someone finds out about the affair, and he imagines the girl to be nothing more than a psycho. When he returns to America, his wife does find out, but she doesn't seem to mind all that much. Neither, it's revealed, does the musician, who, though he tells his wife that "it wasn't anything," concludes that you can't really be too pissed at someone who thinks you are a god, and that there is, after all, "nothing more wonderful and strange than the way men and women manage to get together." [Insert happy music here!]

The three-page "Oliver's Evolution" is even less satisfying. It is the compressed history of a neglected child, who, as a toddler, nearly drowns because his parents, "striving for romantic harmony in the wake of a late party and an alcoholic quarrel," swim off and leave him alone on the beach. It's one of the many occasions when the parents fail to be there for Oliver, and by page two, he's looking like he actually has problems worth telling a story about but—[Insert happy music!]—by the end of page three, he's married with children and it's all good. In this case, there isn't even a real song—just that inserted happiness. If Updike had shown how this painful situation was so beautifully resolved, if he had developed the subtle psychological twists innate in his story, it could have been a wonderful piece. In skipping straight to the happy end, he creates the impression of needing to reassure himself as much as the reader.

I understand this impulse, or at least I think I do—many authors must secretly itch to stop torturing their characters, to spread their arms and give it up, making everything right in the end. In *Rabbit Remembered*, Nelson thinks, "But order and organization must be kept in the world. Ties of affection must be expressed, or nothing holds," and the thought casually reflects one of Updike's great themes: the tension between emotion and order, indulgence and rigor, cruelty and love. In past books, you felt the characters' awkward, sometimes belligerent attempts to negotiate between the two poles, and you felt their disappointment when they failed; you also recognized their pained efforts to accommodate that failure. In glossing over the failures here, I think Updike means to show affection, not only for his characters, but for the reader, even for life. It's an admirable and, I believe, sincere intention. But "affection" that makes light of ugliness and pain is not very deep. Weighted too heavily on the side of indulgence, this new book lacks dramatic tension; if everything's so easily all right in the end, it doesn't matter much what the characters do.

Nonetheless, *Licks of Love* bears the mark of a brilliant and still-engaged mind. As I read it, I kept imagining Updike as a prospector who, having already found enough gold to last a lifetime, is still sifting for the sake of sifting, making the motions in order to fulfill some private need and paying little attention to what's actually in his pan. If this is what he wants to do, he has more than earned it. But as a reader who thinks there is still more gold there, I wish he'd start paying attention again.

2000

Dye Hard: On *Blonde* by Joyce Carol Oates

Blonde is Joyce Carol Oates's novel about Marilyn Monroe, and it is a very easy book to make fun of if that's what you want to do. Monroe's story is a tragic soap opera that has already been set to every soundtrack imaginable, and now here comes a cerebral lady professor to pound it out on her piano.

And I do mean "pound." Norma Jeane Baker's life was terrible and strange, and Oates hammers that home with a vengeance, emphasizing the actress's every moment of degradation and shame. Indeed, the book is a masochistic festival of feminine shame, filled with incidents such as the childlike Monroe being raped in the ass by a sadistic producer for the privilege of trying out for a bit part in his film (*"Scudda-Hoo! Scudda-Hay!"*), for which she auditions with "ugly brown menstrual blood" soaking through her Kotex and a "searing pain in [her] anus." Such things happen, and maybe they happened to Monroe *a lot*. But Oates renders this and countless other moments in a tone of ululating hysteria that is often emotionally pornographic. The ass-raping chapter is called "Hummingbird," and it juxtaposes Monroe's helpless delicacy with the grossness of the action to needlessly heighten the pathos.

"Love me, don't hit me." "Don't make me into a joke ... I beg you." "Could you p-promise not to ... Otto, please!" The Monroe of *Blonde* is an ideal Sadean victim, and Oates places her in a Gothic landscape built of feverish language: "The secret place between her legs had been rent and bloodied and claimed by the Dark Prince." "Never had Warren been so big." "Never would we know." "But no, never will we hear."

I repeat, you can make fun of *Blonde*. You would even be right, except that, even with all the qualities just described, the book has real power, energy and locomotive force reminiscent of Dickens or Hugo—who, if judged by today's standards, would also be deemed hysterical and melodramatic.

Oates's narrative voice here includes three modes: one runs up and down on the surface of the story, nearly incoherent with the horror of what it relates, yet relating it with the silly, affected phrases beginning "Never would ... " Another is the voice employed by Oates the essayist—rigorous, observant, nearly cutting in its precision. The third is muscular and sensual—a stereotypically male voice. The three voices operate independently of one another, creating a rich, clashing jumble. The first one is the strongest, though, perhaps because it has been charged with insistently reminding the other, more sanguine ones that something terrible is happening. That first voice may be high-pitched and theatrical, but it is finally dignified by its genuine grief at the suffering of the fictional Norma Jeane Baker.

Blonde begins when Baker is six, in the clutches of a demented mother whose baroque cruelty toward her daughter is a casual by-product of her own self-destructiveness. The child is sent to an orphanage when her mother tries to kill her and is eventually farmed out to a rough, ignorant farm family, where she is betrayed by the mother who is jealous of her beauty. From a forced marriage to a vigorous young oaf, to a tawdry start in films, to a treacherous menage with two narcissistic bisexual boys, to stardom, addiction, more hollow marriages, a ghastly tryst with the President—along the way, there are too many disasters to catalog.

Oates has stayed faithful to Monroe's life to a great extent, but she has also invented and imagined, infusing the story with her exaggerated sense of degradation that both relies on Monroe's icon status and distorts it. Monroe's some-time degradation at the hands of studios is well-known, but Oates, perhaps out of outraged empathy, is so focused on the star's suffering that she underplays any positive aspect of her beauty, delightfulness and power. Most peculiarly, Oates does not even give the power of Monroe's beauty its due: she repeatedly describes men and boys reacting to the star's nakedness with derisive laughter rather than desire: in one such scene, the teen Monroe is at a swimming pool with some teenaged boys; when her cheap suit gets wet, it becomes see-through. Instead of being struck with eye-popping lust, the boys burst into laughter—hard to imagine! There is little sense of the adored icon about whom Clark Gable said "Marilyn is a kind of ultimate. She is uniquely feminine. Everything she does is different, strange and exciting, from the way she talks to the way she uses that magnificent torso. She makes a man proud to be a man."

But *Blonde* is a novel, and even if it is based on an actual person, it is not bound to represent her literally. Oates's empathy and indignation may be somewhat misplaced, but it nonetheless has the force of larger truth. As a character, Oates's Monroe is viscerally alive, and, with vivid, compelling imagery, Oates makes the reader feel the strength and intelligence that coexists and conflicts with the slutty, manipulative allure, the in-turned rage of her ultra-femme victim. Through this characterization, Oates depicts the American fixation on glamor and ugliness as locked together in a grotesque polarity, feeding off and heightening each other:

> She'd freeze ... she'd walk off the set staggering like a drunk woman sometimes she'd shake her hands at the wrists so hard, it was like a hurt bird trying to fly ... in this shimmering mostly transparent gown they'd concocted for Monroe showing these mammoth boobs & the twin cheeks of her fantastic jelly-ass & the dress dipped low in the back showing the entire back to practically her tail bone ... there was this tragic terrified woman emerging out of Sugar Kane ... like a confectioner's sugar mask melting & its Medea beneath ...

In such passages, Oates's writing is beautiful and clear, and the seriousness of her passion honors her subject. With beauty and clarity, she evokes a world where private and public violently intersect, creating an arena of no safety and no sense; in this unmoored universe, the banal and the infinite crisscross and then run together garishly—as they do in life. Monroe goes to have an abortion, in a car driven by a studio chauffeur:

> The woman with the gloved hands made a face that might be described as a smile-frown. There was a jolting stop. Norma Jeane was made to realize that they had traveled through Time. *Any role for the actor is a journey in Time. It is your former self from which you must depart forever.* A sudden curb! A flight of concrete steps! A corridor and a pungent medical-chemical smell ...

One is given the impression of a soul that has been, by some impossible error, snatched from its deep place in the psyche and thrust into a maze of personality and persona, through which it must grope and blunder, trying to make sense of the earthly barrage of words, images, and ideas like "movie star." The Monroe of *Blonde* is like every other lost soul, except that her lost state is so brutally public; in this essential way, the character may be true to the real woman who continues to touch our imaginations more deeply than can be explained by great beauty and brilliance alone.

When Oates has one of Norma Jeane's lovers describe her sexual style, he could, in a way, be describing the book:

> ... she'd get so excited, so crazed, there wasn't any rhythm to it ... her body was this gorgeous thing she'd stare at in the mirror but it wasn't her exactly, and she didn't know how to operate it worth shit. Funny! Norma Jeane having an orgasm was like stampeding for an exit. Everybody screaming and trying to push out the door at the same time.

Oates's writing in this book can be overexcited, and if you stay detached from it, it's easy to snicker. But if you get caught up in that feeling of everybody stampeding for the door, you forget what you were snicking about—and when she makes it out the door, you're blown away.

2000

It Would Not Be Wonderful to Meet a Megalosaurus: On *Bleak House* by Charles Dickens

I first became acquainted with Charles Dickens in the way I suspect most people of my generation have; by watching various versions of *A Christmas Carol* on TV. It's not a bad introduction. Dickens is fantastically visual and dramatic, full of broadly drawn characters ideally designed to bloom out of the cinematic darkness, their faces glowing with goodness or vice. Many of the film versions do an excellent job of rendering the thematic layer of Dickens's famous novelette—the struggle of good and evil, the purity of children, the redemptive power of charity—and the best ones suggest the deeper layers with their dark cinematography, their earthy depictions of minor characters with their gaptoothed grins and sparse hair standing on end. The 1951 version (starring Alastair Sim) is the most gorgeous film and probably the most faithful to the spirit of Dickens. But it is by pure serendipity that it most wonderfully serves the author: because the film is very old and fragile, weird moving squiggles appear in the primitive dark borders and sometimes even in the shimmering, visibly flickering skin of the stock, the foregrounded figures play out the story against a backdrop that seems to quiver with unseen life, dissolving and re-forming on the margins. This incidentally suggested backdrop, this dark world of teeming movement subtly represents the locus of Dickens' genius—which would be virtually impossible to put into film as we know it.

G.K. Chesterton described the teeming world of *Bleak House* as a kind of literary accident, great because of "the unconscious or *accidental* energy of his genius which broke through at every gap" of the social satire. I don't know if it was an accident—Dickens's prose strikes me as quite purposeful. But *Bleak House* has a fecund ball of life at its core that seems to live independently of its author's purpose, and without it, the story would be a soap opera played by hand puppets. This in itself is not unique; a story is the outer weave, or conscious personality of a novel, but its numinous unconscious—which the reader can feel if not so easily see—is in the secret life that glimmers in the margins or bleeds out from the core. What is particularly striking in Dickens is the contrast between his melodramatic narrative tropes and the protean force that infuses them with kinetic, dream-like power more fully dimensional than psychological realism.

The plot and characters of *Bleak House* are a great busy rattle-trap that would lumber and creak if not driven by this protean force. The overarching social theme is the grotesque nature of the British court system Chancery, introduced in the fantastical first pages, with the Lord Chancellor, droningly addressed as "M'lud," proudly presiding in a filthy city covered in mud, where filthy pedestrians, human, horse and dog, slip and slide in the streets and " ... it would not be wonderful to meet a Megalosaurus, forty feet long or so, waddling like an elephantine lizard up Holborn Hill." Waddling out of this muddy mass comes the generations-long suit, Jarndyce and Jarndyce, through which "whole families have inherited legendary hatreds" and "The little plaintiff or defendant, who was promised a new rocking horse when Jarndyce and Jarndyce should be settled, has grown up, possessed himself a real horse, and trotted away into the other world." Out of it come characters, strange little heads that poke up to yell at "M'lud" and then fall back down, among them a crazy suitor named Miss Flite, bearing her reticule of "paper matches and dry lavender," and two young people, yet unnamed, who will become major characters, Ada Clair and Richard Carstone.

It has been remarked that the glaring legal absurdities satirized in *Bleak House* had ceased to exist twenty years before the book was written; it has also been remarked that it scarcely matters. It doesn't matter because of that Megolasaurus and that rocking horse and that "real" horse, on which a breathing shadow figure leaves this world for the next. These cartoon homunculi—and there are many other throughout the book—extend the life in the novel beyond the frame of the story, in this case back into a cartoon prehistory, then forward into a cartoon death. Like them, like everything in the churning world of these first pages, Chancery is both temporal and forever—a castle made of mud convinced of its eternal nature, its fancy-dressed lawyers and judges acting as hosts for primitive forces of madness and destruction.

Chesterton called the beginning of *Bleak House* "an alpha and omega," and he is right in that it suggests a primeval world seen through the palimpsest of evolved, codified society. It suggests also the contrast between eternal forces and the mortals who live within them—twittering Miss Flite flying by, Tom Jarndyce blowing out his brains in a coffee shop, and "the little counsel with a terrific bass voice" who rises from the fog and then drops back down. ("Everybody looks for him. Nobody can find him.") These contrasts are huge, frightening and comic; Dickens puts the emphasis on comedy, not because he is coarse, but because he is mature in the truest sense of the word; he may have written in part to protest social evil, but he accepted reality on reality's terms. Here is his ghastly slum, Tom-all-Alone's, where crime and pestilence rule:

Much mighty speech-making there has been, both in and out of
Parliament, concerning Tom, and much wrathful disputation how
Tom shall be got right ... In midst of which dust and noise, there is
but one thing perfectly clear, to wit, that Tom only may and can,
or shall and will, be reclaimed according to somebody's theory
but nobody's practice. And in the hopeful meantime, Tom goes to
perdition head foremost in his old determined spirit.

But he has his revenge. Even the winds are his messengers, and
they serve him in these hours of darkness. There is not a drop of
Tom's corrupted blood but propagates infection and contagion
somewhere. It shall pollute, this very night the choice stream (in
which chemists on analysis would find the genuine nobility) of a
Norman house, and his Grace shall not be able to say Nay to the
infamous alliance. There is not an atom of Tom's slime, not a cubic
inch of any pestilential gas in which he lives, not one obscenity or
degradation about him, not an ignorance, not a wickedness, not a
brutality of his committing, but shall work its retribution, through
every order of society, up to the proudest, of the proud, and to
the highest of the high. Verily, what with tainting, plundering, and
spoiling, Tom has his revenge.

On the top layer this passage is a grim moral anthem of social
revenge—deeper down it shows an amoral, gut level affinity for
sheer, rich ugliness, which Dickens the artist could revel in with
childishly amoral freedom.

*

The book is baldly theatrical, almost primitively so, and the main
characters are nearly like playing cards with their static defin-
ing traits: Esther, a pious, good, wise young orphan who narrates
about a third of the book. Ada Clair, a beautiful and angelic inher-
itor of the suit's legacy who becomes Esther's best friend. Richard

Carstone, Ada's cousin and lover. John Jarndyce, a beneficent elderly bachelor who nobly turns his back on the loathsome suit. He becomes the guardian of Richard, Ada and Esther. Sir Leicester Deadlock, a foolish, pompous baronet who "has a general opinion that the world might get on without hills, but would be done up without Dedlocks." He is married to the beautiful, inhumanly cold Lady Dedlock, who "If she could be translated to Heaven tomorrow ... might be expected to ascend without any rapture." Unknown to her husband she harbors a secret that could destroy her, and Mr. Tulkinghorn, a lawyer who works for Sir Leiscester, is on to her and is determined to expose her. Running round these, banging into one another and bellowing, are: the Smallweed family, a malevolent, half-crazed clan of loan sharks. Mr. George, a good-hearted vagrant soldier who owns a ramshackle shooting gallery. Mrs. Jellyby, a phony philanthropist with a filthy house, enraged children and a husband who sits with his head against the wall. Harold Skimpole, a dainty little monster, a self-described "child" who would send a real child to his death. Jo, a miserable street urchin who unwittingly gives Tulkinghorn his weapon against Lady Dedlock. This is a bare list of characters and the mere suggestion of a story that crescendos and crashes like a Puccini opera, all the while careening like *Little Rascals* meets *The Three Stooges*.

Dickens used a method of characterization that would be unthinkable to the hyper-sophisticated modern writer: he tells you exactly what characters are like, not just on meeting them, but throughout the acquaintance. Then he shows you what they are like through description and dialogue. Then he tells you again—and again and again. Most writers could never get away with this; they would simply repeat themselves. On the face of it, Dickens certainly repeats himself; he can use the same ironical, jesting phrase to describe a character several times in a span of pages. But on a more subtle level, Dickens is not repeating.

He is *deepening,* rapidly taking you through layers of images and movement that develop your sense of the character and his world almost non-verbally—an extraordinary thing in a verbal medium.

Dickens accomplishes this by using words to make concepts into visceral pictures, as eloquent and fluid as dream images. The inhuman longevity of Chancery leaps into the physical form of a rocking horse that mutates into a real horse that trots into eternity while mothers become grandmothers and a man blows his brains out, all in the space of two sentences. Emotions, ideas and events become physical and alive, they roar about and won't be confined to the words that have brought them into being; the images made of words transcend words to become something more primal in their effect, and the apparently simple characters become conduits for essential forces which we can just glimpse in these rushing images. In a pedestrian sense some of the characters are too exaggerated to be realistic. In a larger sense they are faithful to the comic reality that we spend our lives as conduits for forces we don't understand, and which form our characters in a sometimes extreme fashion over which we have limited control.

In the chapter "Sharpshooters," two members of the Smallweed family visit Mr. George in his shooting gallery. These characters are morally static; the former will be eternally wicked and grasping, the latter stalwart and plain-spoken. Granddaughter Judy Smallweed so resembles a monkey that, "attired in a spangled robe and cap, she might walk about the table-land on the top of a barrel-organ without exciting much remark as an usual specimen." Grandmother screeches grim nonsense, "like a horrible old parrot without any plumage," and grandfather screeches back "You brimstone pig!" Whereupon he is, by Judy, "shaken up like a great bottle, and poked and punched like a great bolster" until he and his wife resume staring "like a couple of sentinels long forgotten on their post by the Black Serjeant, Death."

They are scarecrow opposites of the tall, broad, jovial George, with his "sounding voice" and "his large manner, filling any amount of room." When the lunatic Smallweeds come to visit George in his shooting gallery, these character traits, while repeated and amplified, become a mad ballet of stasis and movement. Mr. George's man, Phil, has just been declaring his willingness to be hit in the head, shot at, wrestled and thrown as a light weight on George's behalf, while bodily illustrating these activities, culminating with a devoted head-butt. Into this tornado of personality come old Smallweed and Judy, the spiteful geezer borne aloft in a chair, panting and throttling a bearer.

The ensuing dialogue serves to forward the plot, but the continued imagery and manic action drop us into a surreal energy current running beneath it. Mr. Smallweed is constantly poked by Judy, pounced on, shaken up, poked again and prodded while he slides down in his chair and claws the air, squeezes his cap and snarls. His goblin face with its "skittle ball head" looms out of the narrative with exaggerated size, his "nails ... long and leaden, and his hands lean and veinous, and his eyes green and watery ..." These out-sized images and antics do not increase our understanding of Smallweed—rather they saturate the scene with him, like heavy paint cross-hatching a canvas. His character becomes one dark dimension in the multi-dimensional scene which culminates with everyone riding off together like the Keystone Cops:

> Mr. George is quite confounded by the spectacle he beholds from time to time as he peeps into the cab, though the window behind him; where the grim Judy is always motionless, and the old gentleman with his cap over one eye is always sliding off the seat into the straw, and looking upward at him, out of his other eye, with a helpless expression of being jolted in the back.

But Dickens' lesser characters are (too blandly) accepted for their comic eccentricity. Modern readers have a lot more trouble with his major characters, especially the good ones. Esther of *Bleak House*, as the sainted housewife, caretaker and healer of all who would be healed, is so good that, psychologically, she is scarcely believable as a person of either gender. Even Victorian critics, who presumably had a higher tolerance for feminine treacle than we do, complained about her, one gentlemen confessing to a wish that she either do something "really spicy" or shut up and tend the jam-pots. Vladimir Nabokov, in his lecture on *Bleak House*, pointed out that Dickens had to use a banal churchy voice when speaking through Esther—or to force his own voice into the character's insipid mouth. "I must say that despite the superb planning of the novel, the main mistake was to let Esther tell part of the story," he fussed. "I would not have let the girl near!"

It is true that Esther's unrelenting goodness is crude and simple next to the wild imagery and "accidental energy" that electrify the Smallweeds. But I think that's precisely why her voice is not a mistake—why, on the contrary, it increases the novel's power. Esther works in a sense that's abstract and nearly musical: her voice is like that of an operatic singer—a pure, high ribbon of sound that simultaneously pierces and unites the complex "music" of the other voices, images and kinetic movement. It works through the dramatic contrast of light and boiling darkness, and it creates a feeling of ardent expansion in what could otherwise have been an involuted and too-dense mosaic. A character like Smallweed has the density of one who has made his own personality into a baroque lock-box, and there are many such characters in *Bleak House*. An example is the stupid old poser, Mr. Turvydrop, a living gewgaw deformed by his own will, "pinched in and swelled out, and got up and strapped down, as much as he could possibly bear," made into a rhinestone-encrusted whirly-gig of twisted energy. Or the lawyer Kenge, a mechanical wind-up demon, who moves his hand "as if it were a silver trowel, with which to spread the cement of his words on the structure of the system, and consolidate it for a thousand ages." Characters like these pull the narrative into such tight, weird knots that you welcome the smooth expanse of Esther's conventionally idealized nature, even if the writing that comes with it is often cloying.

Esther's conventional point of view also has another function. When Dickens looks at certain wicked or complex characters through Esther's ingenuous eyes, he can perceive their gross faults with naive clarity while pretending (as Esther) not to know what's wrong with them. It's a transparent device, but it nonetheless creates a feeling of openness and receptivity that is almost maternally tender, and which is complementary to Dickens' fierce comic knowingness. This function is most effective in relation to Lady Dedlock, the novel's dark queen. "My Lady" is introduced in a gorgeous onrush of wet, heavy, murky images that echo the primeval world of the first pages:

> The waters are out in Lincolnshire. An arch of the bridge in the park has been sapped and sopped away. The adjacent low-lying ground, for half a mile in breadth, is a stagnant river, with melancholy trees for islands in it, and a surface punctured all over, all day long, with falling rain. My Lady Dedlock's "place" has been extremely dreary. The weather, for many a day and night, has been so wet that the trees seem wet through, and the soft loppings and prunings of the woodsman's ax can make no crash or crackle as they fall. The deer, looking soaked, leave quagmires, where they pass. The shot of a rifle loses its sharpness in the moist air, and its smoke moves in a tardy little cloud towards the green rise, coppice-topped, that makes a background for the falling rain ... On Sundays the little church in the park is mouldy; the oaken pulpit breaks out into a cold sweat; and there is a general smell and taste of the ancient Dedlocks in their graves.

Emerging out of this backdrop, the artifice of her figure is highly charged. Every time she appears it is reiterated that she is perfectly fashionable, gracious, empty and cold. She is an embodiment of social masking, its power and its idiocy. She is also an embodiment of female power and female pain, and she is like clashing cymbals of raw feeling and iron control. Tulkinghorn's pursuit of her has an unmistakable whiff of sadistic desire; he is awed by the perverse strength and courage of her facade, and lusts to strip it from her. The pivotal confrontation between them is rendered with an emotional eroticism more intense for its restraint:

> She falters, trembles, and puts her hand confusedly to her head. Slight tokens these in any one else; but when so practiced an eye as Mr. Tulkinghorn's see indecision for a moment in such a subject, he thoroughly knows its value... He would know it all the better, if he saw the woman pacing her own room with her hair wildly thrown from her flung back face, her hands clasped behind her head, her figure twisted as if by pain.

When Lady Dedlock falls on her knees before Esther, revealing herself in a fury of abjection, Esther's deep, uncomplicated response creates a field of placid receptivity against which the frantic woman becomes more poignant than she might be if Esther was complicated herself:

> Covering her face with her hands, she shrunk down in my embrace as if she were unwilling that I should touch her; nor could I, by my utmost persuasion, or by any endearments I could use, prevail upon her to rise. She said No, no, no, she could only speak to me so; she must be proud and disdainful everywhere else; she would be humbled and ashamed there, in the only natural moments of her life.

The tension is most obviously in the melodramatic emotional juxtaposition of an innocent, loving girl with a perverse, dark woman. But we feel it more deeply as a charged juxtaposition of female elements that have flashed into these painted figures like electricity and animated them. Like the little mortal beings that appear in the huge, grinding morass that is Chancery's introduction, Esther's very banality is affecting and stabilizing against the fierce, surging background that introduces Lady Dedlock and infuses her static character.

But Esther is not always banal. Through her comes some of the book's strangest, nearly mystical perceptions, such as her hallucinatory descriptions of a dangerous fever:

> ... I am almost afraid to hint at that time ... when I labored up colossal staircases, even striving to reach the top, and ever turned, as I have seen a worm turn in a garden path, by some obstruction, and laboring again ... Dare I hint at that worse time when, strung together somewhere in great black space, there was a flaming necklace, or ring, or starry circle of some kind, of which I was one of the beads! And when my only prayer was to be taken off from the rest, and when it was such inexplicable agony and misery to be a part of the dreadful thing?

It is also through Esther that Dickens shows us the harbor at Deal, where she has gone to meet Richard, where the sun makes "silvery pools in the dark sea," and the ships "brightened and shadowed and changed." In those fever visions and in those sunny, silvery pools there is a hint of a world unknown not only to the characters, but to the reader and even to the writer. This world, and the tingling peculiarity of its inhabitants, can be briefly revealed in moments and images which may be amusing or beautiful or terrible but which are finally mysterious. In the context of such a world, we are reminded of our own banality, and our need for the unalloyed goodness that Esther represents.

*

With all the roaring energy he summons, accidental or no, and all the ranting little heads popping out of his fantastic landscape, Dickens is excessive by modern standards. But modern standards have become denatured, and Dickens is excessive like Nature; like living things his creatures must twist and turn, expand out or tunnel in until they have utterly fulfilled what they are. They must bang their tankards on the bar and sing the song, whether it's corny or not. Dickens can have one of them dying a supernaturally horrible death of drug overdose, and then, a few pages later, have an entire neighborhood of them crowding the street to hear of it, singing a popular song of the day about a boy boiled alive in the orphanage soup. It's very entertaining, but it's also faithful to human experience, which indiscriminately mixes trivia with genius, artificiality with raw power, sentimentality and seriousness.

One of the most touching scenes in the novel is the transformation of Sir Leicester near the end. He has been severely humbled by the discovery of his wife's secret and her flight, jeered at by a servant and crippled by a stroke. Society expects him to renounce his wife, but instead, before his household, he declares his loyalty to her with the pomp and bravado that have, until now, made him the novel's chief stooge:

> His formal array words might have at any other time, as it has often had, something ludicrous in it; but at this time, it is serious and affecting. His noble earnestness, his fidelity, his gallant shielding of her, his generous conquest of his own wrong and his own pride for her sake, are simply honorable, manly and true. Nothing less worthy can be seen through the lustre of such qualities in

the commonest mechanic, nothing less worthy can be seen in the best-born gentleman. In such a light both aspire alike, both rise alike, both children of the dust shine equally.

A really tasteful writer would cut everything after the first sentence. I would cut it after the second, which seems to me simply accurate even if the volume is high. But it doesn't matter; even the melodramatic sanctimony of the last part is essential to Dickens' *Bleak House*—to cut it out would be like trying to stop a freight train on a dime.

Nabokov, in his *Bleak House* lecture, wished to hold Dickens "above the sentimental trash" and "theatrical nonsense" of the author's own making. It is a passionate compliment, maybe too passionate—for in wishing to idealize Dickens, Nabokov does not respect him quite enough. Dickens loved sentimental trash and nonsense as much as he loved beauty and rigor, and he had that rare form of intelligent innocence that perceives these qualities on their own terms, outside of conventional hierarchies. He gave each its due, and in doing so created art that was and will remain uniquely his.

1994

Somebody with a Little Hammer: On Teaching "Gooseberries" by Anton Chekhov

Last September I was reading in my Syracuse apartment when something very large thundered down the street and stopped with a loud grinding of gears. I looked up; long pulses of light were coming through the blinds. Parting the slats with my fingers I peeped out; there seemed to be a car parked in the air across the street. I opened the blind and saw that the car was actually mounted on a metal apparatus hauled by a mightily blinking truck cab. As I watched, the driver got out carrying what appeared to be a very large wrench and, stopping at various points on the contraption he had hauled, expertly unfolded it so that it formed a ramp from car to street. It was a fascinating sight, the car like a toy held by a giant robot hand, and I went out onto the sun porch to better see it. There is a park across from me, and from its leafy darkness I noticed several people emerge so that they too could see better.

*

I am an Associate Professor teaching full-time in the English Department at Syracuse University, but I don't live in Syracuse full-time. My husband and I live in Rhinebeck and I commute up on the train. Because I haven't got a car with me in Syracuse, I rent an apartment within walking distance of campus. This means I rent in a building on a block of buildings which caters primarily to students, mostly undergrads whose parents probably pay their rent. (I say they're undergrads because when the school year started and everybody's windows were open, I found myself squeezed between Britney Spears on the left and death metal on the right; if they're not undergrads, something is very wrong.)

Because I walk a lot I am perhaps more aware than some of my colleagues of the frequent "Crime Alert" bulletins that regularly appear via email and posters: many of the muggings, snatchings and assaults occur near my neighborhood. Most sound relatively harmless and inept; many sound very bold, occurring as they do in the middle of the day—for example when a student was pulled off the sidewalk into an abandoned garage and raped this past July. Hearing about these attacks so regularly makes me very aware of my surroundings, which are, for some blocks, broken-down and poor—as are many of the people haunting those blocks, hitting passers-by up for money, or trying to. In cold weather they pretty much disappear, but when it's warm, they're always there. They are especially there in the park across the street from me, a park citizens avoid at night.

I've lived in large cities for most of my adult life—New York, San Francisco and Houston—where large, sometimes volatile homeless populations are the norm, and where the comfortable and the wretched exist together, in some neighborhoods closely so. But to see the same opposites so thoroughly and baldly mixed together in a much smaller city makes me more aware of them, partially because I'm so dutifully informed of every crime that takes place anywhere near me and so continually advised to use the university escort service whenever walking after dark. My awareness makes me feel freshly troubled by the disparity, and strangely, freshly amazed by it. I had been teaching at Syracuse for one semester when Katrina hit the Gulf Coast, and while on one hand the lack of government response was shocking to me, on the other it seemed absolutely congruent with what I saw around me every time I walked to work.

I was thinking of this when I taught Chekhov's "Gooseberries" to an undergraduate class during my second semester. I did not choose the story because I thought it was in any way topical, but the devastation wrought by Hurricane Katrina was fresh in my mind when I chose to read aloud this famous passage:

> Just look at this life: the insolence and idleness of the strong, the ignorance and brutishness of the weak, inpossible poverty all around us, overcrowding, degeneracy, drunkenness, hypocrisy, lies ... Yet in all the houses and streets its quiet, peaceful; of the fifty thousand living in a town, there is not one who would cry out, or become loudly indignant. We see those who go the market to buy food, eat during the day, sleep during the night, who talk their nonsense, get married, grow old, complacently drag their dead to the cemetery; but we don't see or hear those who suffer, and the horrors of life go on somewhere behind the scenes. Everything is quiet, peaceful, and only mute statistics protest: so many gone mad, so many buckets drunk, so many children dead of malnutrition ...

It was towards the end of class and I had to shout over the sound of a jack hammer outside—that may've been why about half the students seemed indifferent. I can imagine too that if they were indifferent (and sometimes it can be hard to know what students feel until they tell you), it was because the passage seemed hopelessly dated, not only in style, but in content. After all, very little now seems to occur behind the scenes except for the exercise of power: images of suffering people have become so routine (I'm thinking of Katrina again) that you can't help but see them even if you don't live in a neighborhood where you encounter them in the flesh. I think, though, that the students' very indifference, if that's what it was, indicates that Chekhov is still right, that no matter what we literally see, on television or in life, we nonetheless will ourselves not to see what we don't wish to see—or to feel. Sometimes too, you don't know exactly what you feel.

*

The night that the car appeared in the air outside my apartment, I had earlier been hit up for money by a ragged middle-aged woman whom I'd seen a few days before, screaming obscenities at some students driving past in a car. I was walking home after having dinner and wine at a student joint, and I was feeling the wine as I opened my wallet. "You are so beautiful," I said a little too expansively. "I thought you were a student when I first saw you."

It was an inane comment; it was also true. Her large, wild eyes were hot blue, and her blond hair was sun-bleached and thick. Her face was regal, even with two front teeth knocked out. Inane or not she didn't care—her eyes were glued to my wallet which she might've snatched if it weren't for the students driving past. "Can I have another dollar?" she asked. "Not today," I said. "But next time. I know I'll see you again." She actually looked at me when I said that.

*

Because she looked at me I remembered her. I wondered if she knew the people who emerged from the park to watch the truck driver climb the ladder on the side of his rig and begin to unbolt the car from its fixed position. I couldn't see them clearly in the dark, and it's possible they were students—but I doubt it. The

153

truck driver got into the car, and drove it down the ramp and into the street, executing a sharp U-turn. One of the people in the park clapped; the others stared at him. The car, looking brand-new and fancy in the flashing light, pulled into my driveway. I said aloud, "You've got to be kidding me!" The driver got out with papers on a clip-board. He stood on the sidewalk for a moment, looking from house to house until a young woman of maybe 19 came out of the building next to me. She looked very pleased to see the car. The driver presented her with the papers on a clip-board; she signed.

"You little fucker," I said. I said it in wonder rather than anger, but I said it. I don't know exactly why. There was nothing horrible or outrageous about the sight of the car being delivered—but I found it ridiculous, irksome and saddening at the same time. Did the girl who had just signed for the car know what a spectacle this was to the people in the park across the street? Did she even see them? Did it make any difference at all that I did?

When I read the speech from "Gooseberries" to my students, I did not finish it. I stopped before I got to the part that expresses an old idea, now very much out of fashion:

> At the door of every contented, happy man somebody should stand with a little hammer, constantly tapping, to remind him that unhappy people exist, that however happy he may be, sooner or later life will show him its claws, some calamity will befall him—illness, poverty, loss—and nobody will hear or see, just as he doesn't hear or see others now. But there is nobody with a little hammer, the happy man lives on, and the petty cares of life stir him only slightly, as wind stirs as an aspen—and everything is fine.

The man who makes this speech is revealed by the end of the story to be an ineffectual, foolish and perhaps envious person, who admits that he can do nothing about the state of the world and implores his younger friends to take action they've no interest in taking. By modern standards, the speech is too simplistic anyway. And yet, in spite of the simplicity and impotence, the reader feels the truth of what is said.

My 19-year-old neighbor may or may not have called herself happy; it seems that very few people call themselves happy now. Arguably, few live at such ease that "trivial daily cares faintly agitate" them. But to me, and I'm sure to the people across the street, she looked the picture of satisfaction as she got into the car and drove it into the small lot behind the building. I continued to watch, fascinated as the trucker methodically re-folded the ramp. By the time he drove away the girl was back inside, and the people from the park were gone—or at least I couldn't see them anymore.

2006

This Doughty Nose: Norman Mailer's *An American Dream* and *Armies of The Night*

1968. "America needed the war. It would need a war so long as technology expanded on every road of communication, and the cities and corporations spread like cancer; the good Christian Americans needed the war or they would lose their Christ."

Private: *Gaitskill first encountered Mailer at the age of 15 when she read Kate Millet's feminist polemic "Sexual Politics." In a special sexism-in-literature section, Millet quoted at length from Mailer's novel* An American Dream, *a vivid comic-book story of society, magic, music, murder, love and sodomy which in Millet's censorious context seemed even more thrillingly dirty than it actually is. At fifteen Gaitskill had a complex streak of practicality which was both cheerful and dour, and which allowed her to retreat into her private cave to thoroughly enjoy Mailer's fantasy as presented by Millet, only to momentarily emerge full of righteous outrage at it; she saw nothing questionable about this.*

When she heard that Mailer would be appearing on The Dick Cavett Show *to discuss feminism with Gore Vidal, she watched, anticipating a full complement of outrage and enjoyment. To her surprise, she was surprised: watching Gore Vidal was like watching a snake in a suit, all piety and fine manners, standing up on its hind tail to recite against the evils of sexism. Before this fancy creature, Mailer was nearly helpless, lunging and swiping like a bear trying to fight a snake on the snake's terms. At one point he spluttered "You know very well I'm the gentlest person here," which made the audience laugh while Cavett and guests made ironic faces—but (horribly enough) Gaitskill sensed that this was quite possibly true, even if Mailer did head-butt Vidal in the dressing room, even if yes, he did foully, and in the dim past, stab his wife at a drunken party. For a gentle person who has been stung by clever, socially armored people adept at emotional cruelty may respond with oafish brutality; it is precisely because he is gentle that he can't modulate his rage or disguise it the way a naturally cruel person can. Gaitskill watched the bear-baiting spectacle with a not unpainful sense of cognitive dissonance dawning in her, both sides of her peculiarly American schizophrenic self finally present and blinking confusedly. The only other person who had aroused such feelings in her before was Lyndon Johnson, whose ugly, profound, helplessly emotional face had made her feel like crying for reasons she could not understand.*

*

Public: In 1967 Norman Mailer took part in a march on the Pentagon to protest the war in Vietnam. He marched along with writers Robert Lowell, Dwight Macdonald and others whom he half-humorously called "notables;" he got arrested on purpose; he wrote a book called *The Armies of the Night*, which won both the Pulitzer Prize and the National Book Award.

The Armies of the Night is part memoir, part history, and as its protagonist Mailer is like a tourist with a rude sense of humor, taking snapshot after snapshot of his grinning, waving, royally urinating self before every possible monument. Royally and literally: close to the beginning of *Armies*, Mailer recounts the drunken, grandstanding speech he gave the night before the march, in which he tried to win back the audience (which, to his angry sorrow, had liked Lowell more than they had liked him) by telling them a story about trying to relieve himself in a darkened lavatory before the speech, where he missed the pot and pissed on the floor. Somehow it is key, this ridiculous speech, which, we understand, was buffoonish, inept, embarrassing— and yet which, in Mailer's mind anyway, was loveable precisely for those characteristics. Every turn of the speech, every nuance of its mood is lovingly recorded with sensitivity, intelligence and wit. Even if you are a woman and so not apt to piss on the floor, it makes you warmly recall the times you staggered into a dark, crowded lavatory and considered relieving yourself in the sink for lack of an available pot. In its evocation of ego-comedy and the commonality of bodily needs, the speech is a somehow poetic introduction to a historical moment of desperate, absurd and whimsical heroism, an attempt by spoiled, life-ignorant, self-infatuated children in romantic revolutionary costume to end a war waged by experienced men of the world—men, as a matter of fact, of Mailer's generation.

Mailer wrote *The Armies of the Night* in the third person style that became his trademark, a droll comment on his public persona which had become so big that, like Gogol's Nose, it sometimes ran around town in fancy clothes, pissing on the floor, picking fights and seducing ladies almost in spite of its (in this case) indulgent owner. "I'm as full of shit as Lyndon Johnson," cried the Novelist, trying to work the crowd that night. "Why man, I'm nothing but his little old alter ego. That's what you got right here working for you, Lyndon Johnson's little old *dwarf* alter ego." *Yes.* "… in the privacy of his brain, quiet in the glare of all that sound and spotlight, Mailer thought quietly, 'My God, that is probably exactly what you are at this moment, Lyndon Johnson with all his sores, sorrows and vanity, squeezed down to five foot eight." *Hell yes!* "This yere dwarf alter ego has been telling you about his imbroglio with the p*ssarooney up on the top floor, and will all the reporters please note that I did not talk of defecation commonly known as sheee-it! ... but to the contrary, speak of you-rye-nation! I pissed on the floor. Hoo-ee! Hoo-ee!"

*

Dream: *Gaitskill was 25 when she read* An American Dream, *and by that time she was ready for it, that is she was in a state of receptivity both dreamy and bruised, a receptivity that understood that life had a top layer with several layers under it, and that sometimes, one bled through the other in strange ways.* An American Dream *is not a diatribe against women or anything that logical; it is not even a realistic novel, but a fluid rendering of archetypal forces, personalized and then stuffed into the social costumes of the time. Kate Millet had, it seemed, crudely, blindly misread the book as a literal rendering, almost seeming to confuse a sexualized fantasy of murder with the real deal. Yet, Gaitskill could see how Millet had become confused. She really could.*

The novel's protagonist, a cock in a person suit named Rojack (or "Raw Jock") is a war hero, author and TV personality, an ex-congressman who meets his wealthy Great Bitch wife ("making love she left you with no uncertain memory of having passed through a carnal transaction with a caged animal") on a double date with "Jack" Kennedy. They are separated and he hates her guts, but still he goes to see her from time to time, and on one of these times she taunts him by reminding him that she does rim jobs for other men. He slaps her, she charges him ("like a bull"), he strangles her and tosses her bitch ass out the window. Feeling great, feeling sexy, Rojack finds and screws his wife's maid, going back and forth between Love's mansion and the place of excrement ("I do not know why you have trouble with your wife. You are absolutely a genius, Mr. Rojack."). Thus refreshed, he goes outside where he meets a nightclub singer (named Cherry) at the traffic pile-up caused by his wife's corpse going splat; Cherry can tell at a glance that he killed his wife, and maybe that's why it's love at first sight.

Yes, the book is driven by outsized fear of and rage at women—for Christ's sake, after the damn wife is dead and lying in her own shit, Rojack is still pissed off at her for being violent and, wishes she would come back to life so that he can smash her nose, kick her ribs in, "kill her again, kill her good this time, kill her right." But even more, the book is driven by a desire to ecstatically swim in the lava of essential forces flowing beneath human life, the raw unknowns of sex and death that animate the endless social masks which charm, blur and bedevil our existence; it wants to catch the winking demon peeping out from between the masks and personalities as they cascade through each and every strange and singular human form. Its attempts to do this—especially the successful ones—are joyous, alive and filled with charged motion even in the stasis of cliché. The different faces he gives to the German maid ("... that mobile, mocking, know-the-cost-of-every-bargain Berlin face, was loose and independent of her now, swimming through expressions, a greedy mate with the taste of power in her eyes and her mouth ...") and Cherry ("A clean tough decent little American boy in her look: that gave charm to her upturned nose tip-tilted ... at the racy angle of a speedboat skipping a wave, yes that nose gave character to the little muscle in her jaw and the touch of stubbornness in her mouth.") are the visions of a faceted eye that enjoys illusions, but seeks to penetrate the core beneath them.

*

Reality: The lava of sex and violence does not run through *The Armies of the Night*, at least not so opulently. This book is about actual people and events which don't lend themselves so easily to archetypal conversion; the shrewd, rational facet of the Novelist's mind was thus called upon, and that must have been a grounding factor. In *The Armies of the Night*, Mailer turns his piercing eye on the anti-war movement, especially Dave Dellinger's tor-tured strategic unification of middle-class pacifists, old-school communists, New Left college kids and hippies chanting to lev-itate the Pentagon, and/or blow smoke up the country's rear. He analyzes the uniquely American wisdom of obscenity and humor, the rhetoric of Hawks and Doves ("He knew the arguments for the war, and against the war—finally they bored him") and flexes his prescient intuition in real-world terms: "There was nothing to fear—perhaps there never had been. For the more Communism expanded, the more monumental would become its problems, the more flaccid its preoccupations with world conquest. In the expansion of Communism, was its own containment. The only force which could ever defeat Communism, was Communism itself."

The Novelist's eye is also richly turned on people, and the book fairly pops with characters: Lawyers in Mad Hatter dialogue with a Jehovahic Commissioner; cops trembling with suppressed emotion; National Guardsmen who are scared to use their clubs but break girls' bones with them; jailers harried by working overtime and college boy prisoners giggling as they taunt them; signifying Yippie monkeys; pure good boys (especially one with the "small bright snubbed features of a cat" who made "the most spectacular arrest ... breaking through the line of MPs ... outrun-ning them, crossing the field on them, doubling back, stopping short, sprinting, loping, teasing them ..."); a Nazi counter-demonstrator and a Marshall with leather testicles in psychic communion: "Join me where the real war is. Already the strongest and wildest men in America wear our symbol on their motorcycle helmets." (Nazi) "Next to strong wild men, you're nothing but a bitch." (Marshall) All of these are full characters, but they are also homunculi, big, small, dignified, ridiculous, jabbering, contem-plative, fine or course textured bits of a whole called America, the book's greatest character, a character rendered half in the rational words of public discourse and half in the language of images and dreams: "The love of the Mystery of Christ, however, and the love of no Mystery whatsoever, had brought the country to a state of suppressed schizophrenia so deep that the foul brutalities of the war in Vietnam were the only temporary cure possible for the condition—since the expression of brutality offers a definite if temporary relief to the schizophrenic. So the average good Christian American secretly loved the war in Vietnam. It opened his emotions. He felt compassion for the hardships and the sufferings of American boys in Vietnam, even the Vietnamese orphans."

And then there is that fuggin Nose, scheming to get arrested and get out in time to make the red-eye back to New York for a glam party with wicked chicks, worrying about the state of his suit, or what the press will say about him, or ruminating obsessively on his first drink of water in prison: "... he took a drink of water. It was characteristic of him to make such a move, and he hardly knew if he did it for the best or worst of reasons, did it because in recognizing the value of thirst he had a small panic to destroy the temptation to search such a moral adventure further, or did he do it precisely because he was now aware of the value of thirst, and so thirst by such consciousness had lost its value since the ability to suffer drought was, by this logic, valuable only if water were not available. Or did he take a drink because he wished to study his new state after satisfying thirst? He noticed only that he was a trifle sad on the first sip, and couldn't stop going to the sink for more and more water afterward, which declared the result of the experiment: between the saint and the debauchee, no middle ground seemed tenable for his appetites."

How bittersweet to read them now, the ramblings of this doughty Nose. They are precious, annoying and narcissistic and yet as such, they are artifacts from narcissism's Golden Age, when the revelation of the self, the man behind the curtain of Art, was a refreshing surprise rather than an especially dull convention.

Compared to today's relentlessly small-focus self-blathering (*of which Gaitskill may herself on occasion be not unguilty!*) Mailer's self-reporting flexibly (a little *too* flexibly in the case of that interminable drink of water) changes the lens of his vision from vast to small in a way that mimics individual perception as it moves from moment to moment, and defuses some of his natural pomposity. It is also (intentionally or not) comically honest about its low motives, its need to dominate and to be loved—especially to be loved by those whom he dominates, for example, the audience of demonstrators whom he called "One big collective dead hass," jeered at for not being black, and generally harangued with drunken nonsense in order to make them—force them—to like him as much as they liked Lowell.

*

Masturbation: *It was not the first time Gaitskill had noticed it, this sore, conspicuous need. In* American Dream, *the evil wife is evil mostly because she does not love the hero, and he is justified in killing her for it; her own daughter from a previous marriage is good in part because she hates her mother for failing to be a good wife to Rojack, and Cherry is an angel for knowing he killed his wife and loving him anyway. When Cherry's previous lover—a black jazz singer insanely named "Shago"—unexpectedly comes to visit, Rojack must prove himself by beating the man until he vomits blood—after which beating, Shago gives it up, the validating approval only a black man can give: "Tell Cherry, her and you, I wish you luck ... I swear. Yes, I swear. Luck, man." To which Rojack (the gentlest man there!) replies, "Thank you, Shago."*

Gaitskill must pause here to recall a conversation she once had with a middle-aged female writer, a paragon of dumpy feminism whom Mailer might've been expected to despise, who claimed, with not uncertain contempt, that Mailer had once not unplaintively asked her "Why don't you like me?" How embarrassing, this need to be liked in a man so free with his fists! How nakedly it appears in An American Dream! *And yet, Gaitskill sensed something more serious embedded in Mailer's maudlin quest and question. If American Dream expresses a wish to be loved by those one beats and kills, it more deeply expresses a desire for union between forces which, in life on earth, must pit themselves against each other, sometimes to the death.*

*

Intercourse: This impulse towards union is more fully developed in *The Armies of the Night* as a wish not only to be liked, but to like; the book is full of emotional turn-arounds in which Mailer will start out dismissing someone, or even loathing him, and then will notice something about him that completely changes his mind: he is able to tell the story of the Nazi kook and the Marshall who subdues him because even though they both appear to loath Mailer, Mailer is able to align himself with them through a convincing preternatural empathy. He considers arguing with a Marxist pedant who is driving him crazy with his incessant lectures, and then decides not to on the grounds that if he won, he would merely "depress the one source of energy in the room."

Mailer's vision of the event is itself a unifying one; as a war veteran, and a hero to a generation which, at least in 1968, largely supported the war in Vietnam, he is someone you might expect to empathize with the marshals and jailers—and he does. You feel his compassion as he imagines how the jailers "... were here to work out the long slow stages of a grim tableau—the recapitulation of that poverty-ridden rural childhood which had left them with the usual constipated mixture of stinginess and greed, blocked compassion and frustrated desires for power," and how the insouciant protestors had not only "... left such careful slow and over-cautious work of reconstruction in a shambles," but were completely unaware that they had done so. And yet he is also able to connect (though not effortlessly; one feels the effort) with the "tender drug-vitiated jargon-mired children" who mounted the offensive on the Pentagon, and finally to respect their rite of passage.

Mailer is able to work this way partly because the same quality that sometimes made *An American Dream* unintentionally funny appears as a strength in *The Armies of the Night*. The problem with *American Dream* is not primarily Mailer's attitude towards women, it is that it insists on taking its big, forceful metaphors and making them literal and physical. It is one thing to create a woman who is emotionally dangerous and verbally cruel, who thus appears intimidating to her husband. However these emotional qualities are treated as if they are physical threats, and under these circumstances, the beleaguered hero *must* kill this woman who is magically made so powerful by malice that he is afraid that, while she is being strangled, she is, from a kneeling position, going to rise up and lift his entire body off the floor. In a novel, this is not a ruinous problem—after all, one of the book's subthemes is magic, and anyway a novel is bound only to obey its own rules. But Mailer stubbornly literalizes his metaphors in essays and interviews too; he says he does not address female writers in *Cannibals and Christians* because a writer can only be judged by whether or not he is able to make the Great Bitch of literature cum like a house on fire—and a woman of course isn't going to be sleeping with another woman!!! He is also well-known for insisting at length in an interview with Paul Krassner that masturbation is equal to suicide, though millions masturbate and live.

(Gaitskill cannot help but note here that it is odd for Mailer to react so strenuously to masturbation. For onanism bears the same relationship to intercourse that dreams bear to reality; in each case the two activities are not comparable and do not compete with one another. If

Mailer the artist seems to confuse the private dream world with prosaic reality, it may be because the dream world, with its layering of symbol, archetype and metaphor, its fluid boundaries between life and death, is where his genius shines most luminously. He only sounds like a kook when he tries to make his poetic, prophetic dreams literal.)

But in *The Armies of the Night,* despite the best efforts of his Nose, he does not overall sound like a kook. This is in part because he seems, in all sanity, to have embraced his kook status, and repeatedly, shamelessly refers to himself as a fool. This is also because 1968 was a historical moment for kooks. It was a moment when a door opened between the worlds of dream and reality, literal and metaphor, and in the strange light that came through that door, the most sober, serious, world-wise, experienced men in power were revealed as kooks—morally wrong kooks. The forces of the preposterous, the romantically costumed, the poetic and the mad were for once right, magnificently right, about the ultimately real question of whether or not a war should be fought. And in that moment, Norman Mailer was the ideal witness, jour-nalist and poet to record their victory in a truer-than-life dream world only he could create.

2009

She's Supposed to Make You Sick: On *Gone Girl* by Gillian Flynn

This is not a book I would normally read; I rarely read mysteries and the title, *Gone Girl*, is irritating on its face. I bought it anyway because two friends recommended it with enormous enthusiasm, and because I was curious about its enormous popularity; the millions of copies sold, the impending movie by David Fincher and Reese Witherspoon, the glowing reviews. I found it as irritating as I'd imagined, populated by snarky-cute, pop-culturally twisted voices coming out of characters that seemed constructed entirely of "referents" and "signifiers," and who say things like "Suck it, douchesnob!" The only reason I kept reading was that, having bought the book in hardcover, I took it with me on a long train ride and it was better than obsessively checking my messages (which *is* something). As I read, I began to find the thing genuinely frightening. By the time the train ride was over, I felt I was reading something truly sick and dark—and in case you don't know, I'm supposedly sick and dark.

The sick and dark of *Gone Girl* by Gillian Flynn is less in the plot (which is a masterpiece of cuckoo-clockwork) than in the vision, especially the vision of Amy, the missing woman. Amy is a beautiful rich New Yorker who is lovely and loveable, at least according to her diary entries, one of which begins "Tra and la!

I am smiling a big adopted-orphan smile as I write this. I am embarrassed at how happy I am, like some Technicolor comic of a teenage girl talking on the phone with my hair in a ponytail, the bubble above my head saying 'I met a boy!'" This boy is Nick, whom she marries, who then loses his job, who pressures her to move to his miserable Missouri hometown, where he reveals himself, according to her relentless chirping prose, as a narcissistic abuser who persuades her to use the last of her trust fund to finance his bar. On Valentine's Day, she buys a gun because "I just would feel safer with a gun."

Meanwhile Nick (chirping in a more masculine register) is revealing Amy as an emotional terrorist who sets baroque, hurtful traps for him, especially on their anniversaries, for which she creates "treasure hunts" full of clues based on shared moments that he can't remember. She goes missing on one such anniversary and Nick quickly becomes a suspect, partly because he's a habitual liar, but mostly because inexplicable, damning evidence keeps turning up against him, including a murder weapon. And then there's the treasure hunt, which appears to be Amy's final love letter, but turns out to be one piece of her final and most malicious trap. The trap has many moving parts, including a faked pregnancy test achieved by harvesting a pregnant woman's pee from a toilet, an actual pregnancy achieved with forgotten frozen sperm, a mysteriously planted stash of porn ("Brutal Anal;" "Hurt the Bitch"), and a faked poisoning backed up by frozen vomit. The few acts of physical violence that occur happen off camera and are not dwelt on. That the emotional violence is rendered in smarty-pants chirping makes it more grating than painful.

What makes *Gone Girl* scary rather than kooky is its cast of characters—what motivates them, and how they view each other. Amy and Nick do not resemble actual people so much as grotesquely smiling masks driven by forces of malevolent artifice, and it's exactly that masked, artificial quality that's frightening to the point of sickening. Most frightening of all is that the artifice is so *normal.*

What I mean by "artifice" is social language, styles, and manners—a public way of being that is by necessity coded, fixed, and hard, and which has become even more so through the emergence of the virtual world. In physical life, the hardness and (frequent) deceptiveness of such language of off-set by the deep, doggishly honest presence of the body; in the virtual world such animal presence is either absent or faked. *Gone Girl* doesn't compare to other books as well as it evokes flipping through TV shows (including the news) and glimpsing face after chirping female face, all with only slight variations on the same manner of speech, facial expressions, and the "smart," high-speed delivery common to Facebook chat, texting, and tweeting; that is to say, the book impressively evokes an artificial hive-minded way of relating combined with what has become a feminine cultural ideal of relentless charm tied to power and control.

This feminine ideal was lampooned/celebrated in the movie *Bridesmaids*, which is about adult women manically competing over things like who will pick the bridesmaid's dresses, who will have the last word in the bridal shower speech, and of course, who has the most and best stuff. The women get food poisoning, shit in their dresses, slam each other in the tits while playing tennis; at the shower, the heroine—who is a quirky single misfit—screeches at the bride about bleaching her asshole whereupon the bride screeches back "I love my bleached asshole!" It's not exactly a new idea: women are filthy, vicious idiots who must compensate with extreme self-control—dress exactly right, talk exactly right, pluck, diet, dye and, hell yes, bleach—then claw at each other/ bond over who is doing it best, and wow, is it ever cute! But *Gone Girl* takes it to a whole other level. Because Amy is rich, beautiful, sharp-witted and thin, she has won the first part of the control game automatically. If you have observed, as I have, that people tend to treat others as they treat themselves, the next natural move in achieving such fanatic self-control would be to control others. This requires a kind of power that most women (and men) do not have—except in power fantasies such as the ones concocted in Flynn's novel.

When I called the friends who'd recommended *Gone Girl* to talk about how sick-making I found it, they both listened in baffled silence before replying "But the character is crazy. She's supposed to make you sick." I guess that by "crazy" what is meant is that Amy lies, manipulates, switches personae, in fact sees herself and everybody else in terms of personae and will do literally *anything* to get her way. But I don't think she's any crazier than the world we live in now. Her meanness—and the unfeeling, appraising way she types everyone she meets—just seems an extreme version of a norm or an accepted cultural language; that hyper-fast hive brain that very nearly precludes seeing beyond a coded surface.

Amy—a paragon of self-possession who always has the last word—constantly typecasts others in the most rigid and nasty way. Here's how she sums up the young woman Nick turns out to be fucking: "Taking his cock in her mouth, all the way to the root so he can feel extra big as she gags. Taking it in her ass, deep. Taking cum shots to the face and tits, then licking it off, *yum*. Taking, definitely taking. Her type would." It's normal, I guess, for a woman to hate her rival. But the hatred and scorn here seem to be not about the competition for Nick's attention; they seem to be about the young woman's (imagined) receptivity or submissiveness—her lack of control.

Amy may be the nastiest, most reductive typecaster in the book, but the reductive tendencies of our cultural moment are part of *Gone Girl's* DNA, and snap judgments emerge without question—particularly at the expense of those who, like Nick's mistress, appear to have less than total control. When Nick and Amy's family set up a Find Amy Dunne Headquarters at a local

Days Inn, a female detective warns him about the rapacious older women (forty-somethings) who will inevitably try to seduce him while pretending to help, and sure enough, one such creature instantly appears. She is, like everyone else in the book, immediately identifiable, in this case by her "Giant brown pony eyes, her pink shirt ending just above crisp white shorts," her "High-heeled sandals, curled hair, gold hoops." Soon she is pawing Nick, offering him pie (!), pouting and complaining that the female detective doesn't like her. Nick responds:

> "Why do you say that?" I already knew what she was going to say, the mantra of all attractive women.
>
> "Women don't like me all that much ... Did—does Amy have a lot of friends in town?"
>
> ... "I think she may have the same problem you do," I said in a clipped voice.

Some critics have called Flynn's portrayals of women misogynist, but to me it seems like she's just amplifying an attitude that's shoved in front of us all the time—on TV, online, in countless tabloids which are constantly informing us that some woman, regardless of age, is "humiliated" because her husband "cheated" or because she gained weight or because, after being dumped by her husband, she had the nerve to get drunk and dance in public— that is, because she did not have absolute control over herself *or* the behavior of her man, and is therefore a legitimate object of derision or pity or both. The book is a representation of everyday cruelties, along with au courant social behaviors and codes that flatten everything and everyone into instant types. Here is Nick being seduced by the supposedly disgusting young lady described above: "... her breasts pushed upward. She wore a pendant on a thin gold chain; the pendant slid between her breasts down under her sweater. "*Don't be that guy*, I thought. *The guy who pants over where the pendant ends.*" Who exactly is "that guy"? A guy who likes to look at women's breasts? Wouldn't that be millions of guys? There is nothing here but "that guy" or "that girl," and that means nothing, period.

There *are* elements to admire in *Gone Girl*: some of the nasty characterizations ring true and Flynn has a witty eye for detail; the intricacy of the plotting is insanely clever. The best and most grounding element though is the backdrop, the small, economically depressed town to which Nick brings Amy, where homeless people live in the abandoned mall at which Nick's mother used to work. The minor characters who populate this backdrop, including Nick's parents, are the only real humans in the book; reminiscent of the "proles" in Orwell's 1984, their "realness" seems to consign them to poverty, illness, wan goodness and small-time criminality—in short, powerlessness. Given this context, rage and annihilating artifice seem a reasonable response, for who would want to be like these people? Amy is just out-playing the hive-mind on its own terms—and winning, on a grand-slam sweepstakes level, all the things the average woman is supposed to want. In this sense, *Gone Girl* is pure black comedy; it is also a maniacal power fantasy that panders to (specifically) female rage and fear. I wonder if "real people" like those depicted by the book are buying it so that they too can enjoy the fantasy, distance themselves from it by calling its heroine "crazy," and then go back to muddling on.

What is unclear to me is how *Gone Girl* regards its nihilistic fantasy. Does Flynn represent Amy's chirping, her charm, and her control over herself and others with a sort of wild, cackling despair? Or does it promote the fantasy, or somehow cut it down the middle? (Perhaps it's unfair to note that Flynn, writing on her blog and the acknowledgments page of *Gone Girl*, sounds exactly like Amy.) Either way, it's difficult to appreciate the book without participating in the fantasy, without living, for a time, in the horrible hive-brain it so successfully invokes. Unlike a TV show, which we can watch while texting, this is written fiction; we have to attentively absorb it word by word. However harsh my comments here, as a writer I can't help but appreciate Flynn's assertion of literature's superior potential to engage readers by subtly making them do more than just listen and watch. But this book seems a little too enamored with Amy's view of the world, and misuses its power in something like the way its protagonist misuses hers.

2013

The Running Shadow of Your Voice: On Nabokov's *Letters to Véra*

We had a pleasant little party the other day, what can I say: tra-la-la, Aldonov in tails, Bunin in the vilest dinner-jacket, Khmara with a guitar and Kedrova, Ilyusha in such narrow trousers that his legs were like two black sausages, old sweet Teffi—and all in this revoltingly luxurious mansion ... we listened to the blind-drunk Khmara's rather boorish ballads she kept saying: but my life is over! While Kedrova (a very sharp-eyed little actress whom Aldonov thinks a new Komissarzhevskaya) shamelessly begged me for a part. Why, of course, the most banal singing of "charochka," a lonely vase with chocolates, the hostess's wail (about me): "Oh, he's eating all the chocolates," a view from the picture window onto the skeleton of the growing exhibition and the moon. *C'etait a vomir.* Bunin* kept impersonating my "arrogance" and then hissed: "you will die alone and in horrible agony."
—Vladimir Nabokov from *Letters to Véra*

In life as in death: if there was a super-hero called Most Loved Yet Most Hated Dead White Male Writer, Vladimir Nabokov could've

---

*Ivan Bunin, Nobel Prize winner of 1933 and very jealous man.

174

THE RUNNING SHADOW OF YOUR VOICE

been buried in the suit. Bring him up in interested company and the reaction may range from snooty, ululating adoration to irrational, pinch-mouthed hatred. For the haters V.N. is an elitist of the worst kind, a contemptuous aristocrat, a probable pedophile, a cruel, immoral, emotionally empty, perhaps *even stupid*, yet freakishly gifted technician with nothing to say. For the ululators (not all of whom are snoots, I'm just acknowledging the royalist fuss-pots on the far end of the spectrum) V.N. is beyond reproach, a moral and intellectual saint who, among other flawless feats, wrote an erotic masterpiece about pedophiliac love purely in order to "exploit the aesthetic possibilities of the material"* or, as the superb scholar Brian Boyd has written with a straight face, to express his "concern for children." Between these two poles there is such a stupefying gap, filled with so much brainiac noise, that when I find myself in such conversations, I become ... stupefied. "Nabokov is cold," coldly comments an academic of my acquaintance. "He's not cold," I answer, "he's hot." "It's finally the same thing," he replies. "There's no warmth." "But he's sometimes even a bit sentimental," I say. "Exactly," is the inexorable reply. "It's false feeling."

In view of all this, I read *Letters to Véra*, a collection of V.N.'s letters to his wife in part with the hopeless hope that *finally* the hater's angrily squeezed eyes could be made to open. That hope is of course irrelevant to the book, which is (to anyone but a confirmed hater) a gorgeous and heartening record of the intimate life of a genius. It is a delightful encyclopedia of pet names (*My joy, floridithy, owlthy, lovethy, my love; my sweet and multicolored Roosterkin*), literary gossip, family stories, lists of boarding house meals (*fried eggs and cold cuts*), drawings of animals, insects and toys, puzzles, opinions on everything from news stories to James Joyce (*Ultimately, wit sets behind reason, and while it is setting, the*

---

*Numero Cinq Vol. IV: *Nabokov's Exoneration* by Bruce Stone.

sky is marvellous, but then it's night) and intense aesthetic appreciations of, among other things, street corners, dachshunds and oil on a puddle (that is, *a huge dullish opal*). Miserly points for the haters: there *are* moments of very petty bitchiness, even towards his admiring friends (the "pink isthmus" between Nina Berberova's two front teeth is made much of) and unpleasant vanity (he seems pleased to scornfully describe an old girlfriend who repeatedly shows up at his readings). When he writes to his wife to indignantly deny an affair he shows himself to be an accomplished liar. However, the overwhelming quality of his letters (which he wrote nearly every day they were apart) is generous, buoyant, sincere and *warm*, most of all to Véra and their son Dmitri (*he still walks all over my soul as if it was his own bed, my darling, my little bunny.*), but also to friends, family, animals of all kinds (the big bad elitist was a great rescuer of mice!), children and yes, even colleagues.

> After tea and still there for dinner (our supper) were Aldanov, Vishnyak (he is very likeable, funny and round), and the invariable Kerensky, who also keeps cracking jokes with a remarkable Jewish intonation, and in general, has mannerisms a little like the old man Kaplan's ... and Mother Maria—a nun, fat, pink, very likeable, the former wife of Kuzmin-Karavaev. And when I, not knowing this, told how Hitlerites had beaten him up, she said with feeling: "Serves him right!"

And then:

> After the meeting, Struve spoke, as well as Kirill Zaytsev, Kartashev (he speaks wonderfully, with tight-shut eyes, with amazing force and imagery), Florovsky and Fondaminsky (who was terribly agitated: they had gotten at *Novyi grad*), with great spirit.

This tone of warm, appreciative engagement with others suffuses the letters; even the snotty passages have an effervescent spirit, for example the one I chose to lead with. And actually the way I quoted that passage is somewhat misleading because I omitted the lead-in to the scene:

> I'm really starting to feel oppressed, the enervating charm of Paris, the divine sunsets (on the Arc de Triomphe, a fragment of the frieze suddenly comes to life—a pigeon taking off), the charm and the idleness, the outlines of time are wobbly, I can't write, I'm desperate for solitude with you …

V.N.'s exasperation at the party didn't spring primarily from his dislike of the company; it seems he much preferred the intimate connection with his wife. He preferred love, which he, in a letter, whimsically described in terms of temperature:

> I have just returned from the Karpoviches, where it was agreeable as always, but also cosy in a new way—a very bright and light house, which has not yet managed (although its starting to, in some corners) to blossom. The water in their tub was, as I told Tatyana, more like (warm) friendship than (hot) love.

The letters create the impression that V.N. temperamentally preferred the heat of love to the warmth of friendship. The need to escape the social nonsense to be with Véra comes up repeatedly and even incongruously; while V.N. was carrying on an affair with an émigré poet named Irina Guadanini, he was literally begging his wife to leave Germany and join him in Paris. This "begging" could've been purely for show, but it does not read that way to me. It suggests instead that V.N., far from cold and calculating, was in this instance not fully in control of himself. His pleas to his wife to come to Paris read almost as if he wanted her to save him.

And she did. Someone told Véra what was going on and she confronted her husband, essentially saying "her or me." He broke off the affair, but continued to exchange letters with his mistress for a couple of months. Guadanini asked to see V.N. one last time. He said no; he had by then reunited with his family in Cannes. She came to see him anyway. She approached him on the beach while he was with his three-year-old son. (She may've come to tell him she was pregnant; afterward she gave birth to a boy she put up for adoption.) He told her that he still loved her but asked her to leave for good. He also asked that she return his letters but she refused. She died—alone and in poverty—in possession of every letter he wrote her and a collection of articles that had been written about him, including some that featured pictures of Véra.

This affair might be seen as an example of what my academic friend was getting at when he said that very hot can be, in its effects, "the same" as very cold—that is, painful. Indeed it seems that the very heat of the affair required a cauterized ending—otherwise, it might've been impossible to end it at all. Guadanini did not simply leave when dismissed. She sat down on the beach some distance from V.N. and Dmitri, and continued to sit there when Véra joined them; she was still there when the family left for lunch.

Few people would want such drama. V.N. truly could not afford it. Like everyone else in the unmoored émigré community, he and Véra (who was Jewish, and often alone with her young child in Weimar Germany), were vulnerable and struggling mightily. The reason V.N. was apart from his wife for such long periods was that he was in Paris and London frantically hustling his work, hand-delivering copies of novels and stories (type-written and posted by Véra from Berlin) to whomever he thought might help him get published, angling for teaching appointments, networking like a fiend. The insecurity of such a life would be hard even in a stable world, and pre-war Europe was brutally unstable. V.N.'s father had been murdered by Russian monarchists in 1920 (they were gunning for someone else when Nabokov senior interfered); in 1939 his impoverished mother would die in Czechoslovakia; later his brother Sergey would die in a concentration camp.

Sergey's story is a particularly painful one; in his memoir *Speak Memory,* V.N. describes his relationship to his brother as "inordinately hard to speak about." Blatantly favored by his parents from birth, V.N. describes himself as "the coddled one" and Sergey as "the witness of the coddling." V.N. was a boisterous and dominant child, Sergey was mild and timid. (A picture of the two boys in 1909 says it all: ten-year-old V.N. is standing with his legs wide apart and his hands on his hips as if inviting the world to adore him on its knees; Sergey, nine, has one leg turned in and his arms crossed over his chest, one finger pensively placed on his cheek.) By his own account, V.N. was something of a bully, although in general he simply wasn't very interested in his brother. He *was* however interested enough (at the age of sixteen) to read Sergey's journal in enough depth to discover that the boy was gay; he was also interested enough to show the journal to their tutor who showed it to their father.

Sergey is mentioned sparingly in the *Letters;* these mentions are heart-rending. In the most striking of them, V.N. quotes at length from a letter his brother wrote to their mother telling her that he had converted to Catholicism because "it is stricter and more demanding than the Orthodox," and because as a Catholic he would be able to "take communion every day" and thereby "kill the sin in [him]," to "make way for something new and not sinful." On quoting this letter, V.N.'s follows with a non sequitur that is unintentionally comic: "I had lunch (veal cutlet, cherry compote) then sailed off (in the chocolate Macintosh) ... " He goes on about his pleasant day for about half a page before breezily commenting "It's true, Catholicism is a feminine arrow-arched faith ... Probably Sergey's carried away by this, but in a good, deep way that will help him a lot."

The response is blithe to the point of—I almost wrote "brutality" but I think the truer word is *incomprehension*. V.N. probably had no idea what it was to feel such anguish and self-hatred, and given that he was trying to create a safe world for his family amid one that was crumbling around his ears, it is hard to blame him for not trying to understand right then. He chose, it seems to me, the survival tactic he was constitutionally best equipped for, that is, to focus on the abiding beauty of the world, in the form of such things as a random cat (... *that special silkiness of short fur, and some very tender white tints on its folds* ...), or the sea (... *very lightly touched up with blue and throwing itself at everything* ...) or any and everything about his wife (... *how I love your handwriting, that running shadow of your voice*). The focus on such small beauties in situations of crushing seriousness can be self-involved and light-minded; it can also be a kind of heroism.

There are comparatively few letters written after the family arrived in America, where V.N. brought his gifts to fantastic fruition. The tone of these letters is somewhat different from those written in Europe; the situational drama and romantic beauty is much subdued, I suppose because the couple was at that point more securely established, materially *and* emotionally. But the quality of lightness and buoyancy remains consistent, suggesting that V.N.'s character seems to have been remarkably independent of external circumstances. The reader of these American letters also hears a refrain of that perhaps *overly* light breeziness when faced with the concerns of people suffering from problems outside his immediate comprehension. On a visit to Spelman College in Atlanta ("a black Wellesley") he notes that "My lecture about Pushkin (Negro blood!) was greeted with almost comical enthusiasm," and expresses good-humored condescension toward a professor who was, in V.N.'s opinion, ridiculously preoccupied by whether or not Pushkin's African descent was "openly discussed" in the Soviet Union. Given the time and place, worse attitudes were possible, and it is true that V.N. had the same condescension towards white people who wished to see their political concerns reflected in literature. But lack of comprehension in this case was not due to any kind of survival reflex or lack of time to stop and think.

It is a questionable project to analyze a writer's personality based on the fiction he has written, or to cross-examine his fiction based on information about his life. Letters, however, are much more naturally revealing. *Letters to Véra* presents neither an elitist prick nor a sainted artist; written with easy grace and sometimes ardent haste, they display rather an artistically spectacular but morally ordinary human being who's gifts and flaws were both thrown into high relief by his transcendentally expressive genius. They also show a man of *unstoppable* energy and joy.

Letters winds to its end with anecdotes about reading tours at small colleges, slap-stick mishaps at train stations, oddball characters and the grotesque customs of the segregated South. My favorite though is about V.N.'s hospitalization for appendicitis in 1944:

> The nurses constantly tried to pull open the curtains of my coop and got angry saying that since all the other curtains were pulled, my poor tabernacle was spoiling the general look of the ward. By the end of my stay I was in such a state of exasperation, that when on Saturday morning I saw from the gallery (where I had gone out for a smoke) T.N., who'd come for me, I jumped out through the *fire-escape* as I was, in pyjamas and a dressing-gown, rushed to the car—and we were already moving off, when the absolutely enraged nurses ran out—but they couldn't stop me.

They still can't.

2016

I Cannot Get Out, Said the Starling: On *Lolita*

"This love was like an endless wringing of hands, like a blundering of the soul through an infinite maze of hopelessness and remorse." (p. 210, *Pale Fire*)

This could be Humbert Humbert agonizing over Lolita after he has ruined her life and his, but it is not; it is Charles Kinbote, King of fabulous Zembla, musing with wistful off-handedness about his young, beautiful, unloved and undesired wife, Disa. In waking hours he feels nothing for her but "friendly indifference and bleak respect;" in his dreams, these dry sentiments are saturated and swollen until they "[exceed] in emotional tone, in spiritual passion and depth, anything he had experienced in his surface existence." (p. 209, Pale Fire) In life he casually, near-accidentally tortures her; in his dreams he remorsefully adores her.

In Pale Fire, Disa is a minor character who receives only a pathetic handful of the book's 214 pages. But with the poignancy and plangency of sorrow, she illumines Pale Fire's core; the delusional dream, the preposterous poem, the crumbling bridge between mundane reality and fantastic ideal, the tormenting ideal which insists on bleeding through to the surface ("all peach syrup, regularly rippled with pale blue" (p.

210, Pale Fire)) *even as it sinks in the mud below. If Kinbote, though King, can't have the one he really wants, Humbert Humbert can: in Lolita the dreamer is in the driver's seat, reality is broken and it is the raving dream that broke it. Humbert "seldom if ever" dreams of Lolita, even when he has lost her. Except that he does. In his grossly unbeautiful dreams, Lolita appears as Charlotte, her disgusting mother, and as Valeria, Humbert's equally disgusting former wife, both of whom disgustingly loved him:*

> ... she did haunt my sleep but she appeared there in strange and ludicrous disguises as Valeria or Charlotte, or a cross between them. That complex ghost would come to me, shedding shift after shift, in an atmosphere of great melancholy and disgust, and would recline in dull invitation on some narrow board or hard settee, with flesh ajar like the rubber valve of a soccer ball's bladder. I would find myself, dentures fractured or hopelessly mislaid, in horrible chambers garnies where I would be entertained at tedious vivisecting parties that generally ended with Charlotte or Valeria weeping in my bleeding arms and being tenderly kissed by my brotherly lips in a dream disorder of auctioneered Viennese bric-a-brac, pity, impotence and the brown wigs of tragic old women who had just been gassed. (p. 256, Lolita)

I must've read Lolita five times before I even noticed this hideously gorgeous paragraph, this miserable aside linking the fatally despised women with the fatally desired girl. Part of Lolita's power is in its extreme oppositions: Even Humbert's fanatically one-directional desire for little Dolly is made more delicious by the sharp tonal oppositions in her "two-fold nature," the "tender dreamy childishness" and "eerie vulgarity, stemming from the snub-nosed cuteness of ads and magazine pictures," the "exquisite stainless tenderness seeping through the musk and the mud," (Lolita, p. 46) of her female being—really, of any being. The tension between Humbert's near-erotic revulsion for women/his miasmic desire for girls, his human despair/his demonic joy, is even more intense; the dream which tragically joins these poles suggests that one has been a palimpsest for the other all along.

*

I wrote these paragraphs in 2013; they are the beginning of an essay about *Lolita,* specifically about the stupendously varied covers between which the novel has lived since its publication in 1955. These words came very naturally to me then; it did not occur to me that I should perhaps not lead with a quote from *Pale Fire* about secret love linked with emotional abuse, and then link it further to literature's most famous pedophile/murderer. It *would* occur to me now because although *Lolita* is (the last time I looked) still being billed with the blurb "The only convincing love story of the century," the idea that a pedophile might love the target of his obsession is, to put it mildly, very out of style. Then there is the matter of tone: like many Nabokov super-fans do when writing about His Majesty, I seem to be mimicking His Eminence with an extra-frothy, slightly preening and alliterative voice. I refer to such phrases as "... with the poignancy and plangency of sorrow ..." and "... Humbert's fanatically one-directional desire for little Dolly is made more delicious by the sharp tonal oppositions in her 'two-fold-nature' ..." The syntax isn't *that* different from one of my more usual styles, but it is different enough that I might look at it and ask myself, why did I want to align my voice so completely with another, more culturally and artistically powerful voice than my own? And I can easily imagine that someone else might more prosecutorially ask *"Excuse me?* You think the pedophile's desire is made *'more delicious'* by ... what exactly?"

My own question is easy to answer: *I was just being playful and okay, it's a little foolish, but who wouldn't want to align themselves (for just a minute!) with something so beautiful?* But there is tone, and then there is content, and the two *appear* to clash so mightily here that my answer might further aggravate indignant possible askers of the second question, who, while they have always been present, are now out in such force as to be positively intimidating. Because they are intimidating, I was tempted to concede here that such a question is legitimate. But in truth I don't think it is. If Humbert Humbert were a real person, I would be outraged myself at the characterization of his desire as "delicious." But he is not a real person. He is fictional, that is, he is an intense illusion, an artful imitation/vector of thought, instinct, feeling and physical phenomena so flawlessly made that we respond to him as if he were actually a human. But he is not. And so my answer would be that yes, Humbert Humbert's desire, its extremity, its piercing-ness, the fever-dream of it, attended as it is by delirious images so startlingly wretched and sublime *is* delicious to me— not only delicious but powerful and profound in its unification of impossible oppositions, most strikingly Humbert's misogynist loathing combined with his perverse need to adore—to love. For me, this is the crux of it, expressed so freely in that blurb taken from a 1986 review in *Vanity Fair* by Gregor von Rezzori: "The only convincing love story of the century." I don't think that *Lolita* is a "love story," primarily because that phrase suggests mutuality. But I do think that it is in part about love; love that is broken, or simply misshapen by adapting to some kind of incomprehensible fate, subliminally shaded with fear and humiliation and rage that have nothing to do with the loved one. Indeed that was the main thought behind the essay I wrote in 2013. It did not occur to me then that I should "defend" such thoughts but it does occur to me now, or it did when a friend, to whom I described this essay somberly remarked "you're going to have to defend that." However, before going there, I want to, as they say, *contextualize*.

In 2020, it may not be necessary for me to say who I think my hypothetical "indignant" asker of a "prosecutorial" question might be, but for the sake of clarity, I will do so. They are collectively the millions of pixels that make up the towering #MeToo movement, which has become the #MeToo era, the "Afterlife" referred to in the title of this book. Also for the sake of clarity: while I have mixed feelings about #MeToo I believe it has often had a salutary purpose and effect. It exists to correct social and legal crimes committed by actual people, and while it's a real problem that its soldiers sometimes fire so wildly that they shoot dead the occasional harmless weirdo or raw romantic, they have stopped some real assholes in their tracks.

But to state what should be obvious, just as Humbert Humbert is not a real person, art is not real life; it is a categorical error to look at the author of a novel or a character in that novel in the same way you might look at, say, a vicious twit advocating white supremacy plus male supremacy plus sex with underage girls on a right-wing website. (I am, unfortunately, not making this up; I'm referring to a website called Heartiste, which was yanked down maybe a year ago after a long, hideous and hilarious online tenure.) Yet this is essentially what some ardent feminists/moralists have done or tried to do, for example, the sisters who, in 2017, circulated a petition, signed by thousands, demanding that a painting of a young girl (*"Therese Dreaming"*) be removed from a Balthus retrospective at the Met in 2017 on the grounds that it is "suggestive." (To call *Therese Dreaming* "suggestive" is a ridiculous understatement; it is bluntly sexy. It portrays a young girl sitting with her face turned up and to the side, eyes closed as if in reaction to a combination of bright, hot sun and bright, hot thoughts; her arms are behind her head, her legs are open and one knee is up, showing her white underpants. She is distinct and small and saturated with impersonal force that she appears to bask in, and you feel the depth and breadth of this ordinary moment.)

The insistence that art be moral is as old as dirt: *Madame Bovary* was deemed "an outrage to public morality" in 1857; Nabokov spent decades defending himself from the charge of creating a comical child molester; his scholarly fans have since labored to exonerate him from said charge on sometimes very esoteric grounds, for example, that *Lolita* isn't actually about pedophilia at all but is rather about ... time.

But #MeToo has given this ancient argument new force and omnipresence. It has also gendered and politicized it. It has very possibly affected my reading of *Lolita* almost by osmosis. It is true that when I first read the book at age 23 I did not focus on the plight of the exploited girl. I was aware of it as a major aspect of the story and I was aware that it was a moral wrong—indeed the fact that I took it for granted as a moral wrong made it less dramatically interesting for me, for if it is obvious to you that something is wrong, why read a novel as if it is written entirely to illustrate the wrongness of it for you? But it was in any case not where my attention was most of the time. Mostly I was tuned into Humbert's point of view because he was telling the story and because his voice was one that I could I identify with through the force of his observations. By "observations" I don't mean his opinions or ideas, I mean his ability to look at and transform the world—say, a hotel lobby, a stand of trees or a retail outlet:

> There is a touch of the mythological and the enchanted in those large stores where according to ads a career girl can get a complete desk-to-date wardrobe, and where little sister can dream of the day when her wool jersey will make the boys in the back row of the classroom drool. Lifesize plastic figures of snubbed-nosed children with dun-colored, greenish, brown-dotted faunish faces floated around me. I realized I was the only shopper in that rather eerie place where I moved about fish-like, in a glaucous aquarium. I sensed strange thoughts form in the minds of the languid

ladies that escorted me from counter to counter, from rock ledge to seaweed, and the belts and the bracelets I chose seemed to fall from siren hands into transparent water.

I did not have at 23 the vocabulary or the skill to describe a scene like this, but I viscerally recognized it as potentially one of the many weird and quotidian mall-shopping experiences of my teen years. The language was impressive but to me it was also affirming and, most remarkably, seemed natural to the author. How wonderful that such a thing could exist!

Perhaps because of #MeToo, I *have* recently wondered if my identification with Humbert's voice was a kind of unconscious and acculturated alignment with the masculine point of view which I had come to see as perforce the most interesting one, to the point that for a long time I only secondarily absorbed Lolita's half of the story. I think there is something to that, though certainly most male narrators do not automatically compel me. I have wondered more about my stylistic mimicking of Nabokov's voice when I write about him. It is maybe inevitable for an artist to be influenced by art that she admires, and natural to playfully flaunt it. But the beauty of Nabokov's art is *powerful,* and to borrow someone else's artistic power through mimicry is artistically weak. But I'm not sure that this kind of delighted weakness towards something that has nourished you is always a bad thing. Especially as a young person, Nabokov's language gave me a kind of mental nourishment and confirmation that I did not often find, as a human being rather than specifically as a writer—and I'm sure I'm not alone in that.

I don't doubt this declaration makes some people want to throw this book across the room! Hostile critics have repeatedly used the beauty of Nabokov's language against him, claiming that it is a screen or a distraction from what is "really happening," or a means to make you "complicit" in Humbert's crimes; well before

#MeToo, Calvin Trillin among others worried this worrisome idea, and Trillin was a fan of the book. The language of *Lolita*, in the voice of its "dog-eyed gentleman," (p. 88, *Lolita*) may be a lure and a distraction, but it is also something else: this language and the world created by it *is* what is "really happening," and is equal in importance to the story line.

> ... those elementary rusticities became stranger and stranger to the eye, the nearer I came to know them. Beyond the tilled plain, beyond the toy roofs, there would be a slow suffusion of inutile loveliness, a low sun in a platinum haze with a warm, peeled-peach tinge pervading the upper edge of a two-dimensional, dove-gray cloud fusing with the distant amorous mist. There might be a line of spaced trees silhouetted against the horizon, and hot still noons above a wilderness of clover, and Claude Lorrain clouds inscribed remotely into misty azure with only their cumulus part conspicuous against the neutral swoon of the background. Or again, it might be a stern El Greco horizon, pregnant with inky rain, and a passing glimpse of some mummy-necked farmer, and all around alternating strips of quick-silverish water and harsh green corn ...
> (p. 152, *Lolita*)

Behold the natural world that we see before us every day and barely notice; it is indeed miraculously strange to the eye the nearer you get. In terms of objects, color and phenomena (clouds, roofs, trees, corn), the description is realistic, poetic and piercingly accurate. It is also wildly alive, filled with movement and whole worlds, invisible to us, that bleed in and out of the imagery in various guises, for example that tiny mummy that is also an unsuspecting neck. It is suffused, it is amorous, it swoons, it is pregnant, the corn is *harsh* and countless segments of time (noons) are suspended above a wilderness made up of humble weeds. This *vastness* is joyful and unknowable in its protean raiment, and it unscrolls with limitless fecundity throughout *Lolita*: a beautiful young girl glimpsed through a "jewel-bright window" as she combs her Alice-in-Wonderland hair becomes an "obese partly clad man reading the paper," (p. 264) and Humbert bays through the undergrowth of Mama Haze' "dark decaying forests" in despair; (pp 76–77) his human heart feebly tries to assert itself between two tiger beats, (p 111) a "haggard angel" regards him from behind Lolita's shoulder (p 125) and dead Charlotte rises from her grave from the mist of her daughter's cigarette smoke. (p. 275) The novel's intense pattern of images, coincidences and puns suggests "a marvelous system of spells and wiles*" that mimics the complexity of the natural world which shapes our lives and sometimes moves us without our knowing it. In this humorous, fast-moving and multi-valanced system, so innocently lovely and weirdly sinister, characters (Mrs. Haze, Dolores plus Humbert) strive with all their tiny might for some kind of agency and goodness and joy, ardently, ludicrously, pitifully, selfishly and with desperate amorality collapsing into evil—as real humans do. Truly, the darkness—the cruelty—of the story is not obscured but *heightened* by the beauty of the language through the force of artistic contrast, and that contrast is stunning, making the reader feel the wild, often terrible incongruity of human life on earth. This incongruity—the natural coexistence of beauty and destruction, goodness and predatory devouring, cruelty and tenderness, "the torturer's horse scratching its innocent behind on a tree"†—is a core mystery of life. And that mystery is the true heart of *Lolita*.

Back to the idea that *Lolita* is about love; this is what I wrote in 2013:

---

*An expression used by Nabokov in the preface to his Lectures On Literature (p. 5).
†"Musee des Beaux Arts," Auden.

But the blurb on [the] cover is more disturbing than the image, for it sincerely states that Lolita, *in which the heroine is seduced, kidnapped and grossly used, her mother humiliated at length before dying violently, the seducer himself shattered, his rival murdered, the heroine finally dead along with her "still-born baby girl"—according to the blurb, this madcap orgy of Thanatos, is "The only convincing love story of the century"!!!! It is not shocking that someone said this, especially given that this someone was Gregor von Rezzori writing for* Vanity Fair. *But it is quietly outrageous that a mainstream publisher would choose to put it on the cover ... for how could anyone call this feeding frenzy of selfishness, devouring and destruction "love"? And yet, consider what Nabokov said about Humbert: that while he, the author, would condemn his character to hell for his acts, he would allow Humbert, for one day a year, to leave Hell and wander a "green lane in Paradise," and that this parole would occur because of the glowing particle of real love he bore Lolita.*

Although I find Rezzori's words initially repellent and even a little smug, if you rewrite the sentence without the words "only" and "century," I have to agree with them. Lolita *is about obsession and narcissistic appetite, misogyny and contemptuous rejection, not only of women, but of humanity itself. And yet. It is also about love; if it were not, the book would not be so heart-stoppingly beautiful. Here is Humbert on finding his runaway sex slave, now married and pregnant at 17:*

> *You may jeer at me and threaten to clear the court, but until I am gagged and half-throttled, I will shout out my poor truth. I insist the world know how much I loved my Lolita, pale and polluted and big with another's child, but still gray-eyed, still sooty-lashed, still auburn and almond, still Carmencita, still mine ... even if those eyes of hers would fade to myopic fish and her nipples swell and crack, and her lovely young velvety delicate delta be tainted and torn—even then I would*

go mad with tenderness at the mere sight of your dear wan face, at the
mere sound of your raucous young voice, my Lolita. (p. 281, Lolita)

This is love crying with pain as it is crushed into the thorned corner
of a torture garden—but it is still love. Purity of feeling must live and
breathe in the impure gardens of our confused, compromised, corrupt
and broken hearts. Love itself is not selfish, devouring or cruel, but
in human beings it suffers a terrible coexistence with those qualities,
as well as with a host of milder evils—say, resentment or jealousy or
misunderstanding or projection. These oppositions sometimes coexist
so closely and complexly that the lovers cannot tell them apart. This
is not only true of sexual love, but of the love between parents and
children, siblings and even friends. In most people this contradiction
will never take the florid form it takes in Humbert Humbert. But such
impossible, infernal combinations are there in all of us, and we know
it. That Lolita *renders this human condition at such an extreme, so*
truthfully, and yes, as Rezzori says, convincingly, is the book's most
shocking quality. It is why it will never be forgotten.

I don't know if I can "defend" these words or if I want to. They
seem so obvious to me that it's hard for me to understand disagreement with them. But I suppose agreement or disagreement
would depend on what you mean by "love." To me love primarily means an emotion. It might be a tender, gentle emotion or a
mutually devouring emotion (think *In The Realm of the Senses*,
the 1977 film by Nagisa Oshima). It might be both at different
times in the same person (think *Song of Solomon* by Toni Morri-
son). When we say "love" we might include experiences that we
can't explain even to ourselves, except that it felt wonderful. Or
horrible. I know many people would say that if it felt horrible,
or if it isn't mutual, or if it made you behave badly that it "isn't
really love." But I don't know how anyone can be so sure, in such
a clear-cut hygienic way, of what someone else feels. I am not

different from most people; when I think of love, I first think of
it in its ideal state: a feeling of joy in someone else's presence,
a feeling that bathes even the most unpleasant traits in a glow
of understanding and forgiveness, the wish to make that person
happy, the simple wish to rub your face on their face. If we are
lucky we *do* experience love in its ideal state at least some times
and it is the most wonderful feeling there is—but like all feelings it is highly changeable and the deeper and more intimate it
becomes the harder it is to negotiate (as in negotiate a terrain,
not a bargain) because it has more layers. It becomes attached
to other emotions and traits that we are not really aware we had
until we are acting them out in ways that we sometimes have
inadequate control of. It makes even the strongest person terribly, uniquely vulnerable, and for that reason the same people who
long for it can be actually afraid of it. Everybody treats people
they love badly sometimes; everybody hates the people they love
sometimes, or behaves aggressively towards them. To paraphrase
Humbert, sometimes a passionate dream overshoots the mark
and plunges into a nightmare. That is why the idea that "marriage
is hard work" is a cultural given; the ideal state cannot hold on a
daily basis.

Humbert Humbert is not capable of even a grossly flawed marriage and his "ideal state" is a perversion. But even if his ideal is
warped (in part *because* he wants to hold it in a falsely static place
of unchangeable youth and perfection) it is nonetheless how he
can imagine love in the only way he knows how. He comes to
his "tiny particle" of it in reverse gear; at the beginning what he
experiences as love is almost completely blind to the humanity
of its object whom he loves as he might love an especially nice
dessert; as the novel progresses he slowly, as his occluded heart
allows, comes to see her as she really is and to *respect* her wishes
even as she rejects him. This respect, more than the emotional
language, is what convinces me that his particle of love is real. I'm

sure books have flown across the room by now but still I contend that this artificial monster, this vector, this non-human figure of art has a great deal in common with us humans whether we are male or female or non-binary, even if we have never had a pedophile impulse in our lives; that is possibly the most offensive thing about him.

And some of us also have a great deal in common with that other figure of art, Dolores Haze. There are women who, having experienced seduction or even assaultive relationships by and with older men—men who said and who may've meant that they were in love—especially revere *Lolita*. Their reasons must vary, but I think I understand them on a basic level. I think this because of my own experience of molestation at the age of five—yes, me too. The connection may not be obvious; the psychology of a five-year-old is very unlike that of a teen or pre-teen. The man who molested me lived down the street from us with his wife and young son. He also worked with my father and came to our house often. I doubt that I thought about what he felt for me; I probably thought he liked me because he wanted to take me to the park a lot. I had no ability to analyze that kind of thing or to understand what was happening. But nonetheless, I knew that *he* knew he was doing something wrong; I could see it in his face. And I felt, to a shocking and bewildering degree, that he was driven to do it anyway, driven by *something* that, right before me, turned him into *something* unrecognizable, a creature full of hunger and pain and shame that I absorbed into my body. And that, when it was over, he returned to himself. Because of my age I don't remember many details or even how many times these things happened. I do remember that they happened in a public park, in daylight, that his son was sometimes present, and that at least once, although we must've been hidden from view, I could hear the faint, light-hearted sound of people's voices on the wind. I trust these memories because my mother corroborated that he sometimes took me out to the park, sometimes with his son, who was my age. She also corroborated that I told her what had happened at the time and that she did not believe me because she couldn't believe that a family man would do something like that.

It was precisely this, because he was a neighbor and family friend that I trusted him. He never physically hurt me and so I was never afraid of him, not even when he transformed into a different person in front of me. I was stunned but not afraid. Because I had no fear I had no defense against my body's sexual feelings and I got very aroused. I had no defense against my child's natural empathy and so along with feeling arousal I also felt his suffering, which was immense. I don't mention his suffering as an excuse; no one should have someone else's pain acted out on them like that, let alone a five-year-old. I am just stating a reality. I know that this man killed himself some years after he molested me. But even if I didn't know that I would know that he suffered because I felt it; felt it and bonded with it.

(Let's pause for a moment. I realize this might be an awful thing to read; it's an awful thing for me to read. It feels incongruous to write about it in an essay on a work of art, and it may be unpleasant to read, even nauseating. If so I am sorry—I mean that. But I can forget how unpleasant it is because it's something that, like Humbert H, like a great many actual people, I live with all the time, along with the standard concerns of daily life. So let's pause to acknowledge all of that. Now, back to the essay.)

Perhaps because of this experience I have an unduly empathic response to imaginary Humbert's imaginary feelings. Perhaps I am practicing—even as a reader!—some antediluvian survival strategy that I have practiced for a very long time, some complex Stockholmian response to a much-too-early encounter with evil in ordinary life—in the park, in the sun, among families. I can't know for sure; when I say "perhaps" I really mean "perhaps." But I can know this, that on reading *Lolita* I loved it in part because

I was deeply satisfied and even comforted by its rare acknowledgment of the awful complexity of the human relationship to beauty and evil, normality and evil, even love and evil. I wasn't tricked into this by the use of "fancy words"—one of the more bone-headed terms used to dismiss Nabokov's style—or anything else; I recognized it, intuitively, before I even knew what I was recognizing. I recognized it especially at the end of *Lolita* when Humbert begs Dolores to return to him. She says "No. No, honey, no." He notes, piercingly, that "She had never called me honey before." The scene is piercing because we feel her compassion for him—but it is compassion tainted with woundedness, arising as it does from her unchosen proximity to her kidnapper's pain, where her child's natural empathy was tragically linked with her own victimization, the injury to her will.

It is also perhaps because of this experience that I am agog at well-meaning attempts to defend Nabokov from moralizing haters with arguments that *Lolita* isn't really about pedophilia, that the subject of pedophilia in the book is actually a metaphor or an intellectual construct. Bruce Stone's online essay "Nabokov's Exoneration: The Genesis and Genius of Lolita" is an elegant and eloquent example of such an argument. After spending pages on the various moralistic arguments against the book (including "arguments" made by a group of Russian zealots who hurled bottles through the window of the Nabokov Museum in St. Petersburg and beat a theatre director), Stone finally comes to his own point of view which I will try to fairly represent out of context:

> As I see it, the real subject of *Lolita*, its proper theme, is not immorality but immortality ... Humbert's pursuit of nymphets, his longing to reside on that "intangible island of entranced time," appears to be a crazed instantiation of a larger existential crisis ... the novel's treatment of pedophilia is, by definition, *philosophical* and *aesthetic*, rather than practical ... Nabokov portrays the subject

as filtered through the prism of art to exploit neither readers nor victims of the crime, but the aesthetic possibilities of the material. To that end, Humbert's obsession is figured as a crisis of the artistic imagination, which loosens the boundaries between fact and fiction, unmoors time from its anchor; nymphets and their mythical island don't exist, but Humbert deceives himself into believing that they do—and this is a recipe for tragedy.*

I absolutely agree that the wish to suspend time, to "entrance" it, to make a realm immune to its passage is a deep theme of the book. (Nabokov, via Humbert, says as much on page 264.) I even think that a fanatic infatuation with youthful beauty has that "existential" urge to it alongside ... another kind of urge. I even think that the will to suspend time has an element of psychic violence to it—an arrogant desire to defeat the simple fact of our mortality—that is not by itself pedophiliac in nature, but for which a story of pedophiliac lust is a perfect metaphor. But. It seems absurd to assert that anyone's treatment of pedophilia may be "by definition philosophical." The subject is simply too deep, too raw and too savage. And while it may be unfashionable and/or unpleasant to say so, the desire for very young girls is also common, as is Humbert's loathing of mature women—common and far too visceral to speak of in purely aesthetic terms. In spite of the horrified tut-tutting on the part of male critics, it is obvious that many men have some combination of these feelings to one degree or another even if they don't act on them; if they did not, *Lolita* would not have become, in spite of its literary gravitas, a decades-long world-wide ribald joke. On top of its thematically integrated aesthetic beauty, what makes *Lolita* powerful is its combination of intellectual force with lurid, amoral id-force, acknowledging the

*pp. 10–11, Nabokov's Exoneration, May 1, 2013, NumeroCinqMagazine. com.

peeping monster face (surprise!) of our own nature with horror and humor both, as it stands there in the sun "his hirsute thighs dripping with bright droplets, his tight wet black bathing trunks bloated and bursting with vigor where his great fat bullybag was pulled up and back like a padded shield over his reversed beast-hood." (p 237, *Lolita*). The "monster" (arch-fiend Clare Quilty) is masculine here, but he certainly has his feminine correlate; just as Dolores' mother hopelessly loves Humbert, Dolores herself loves the disgusting possessor of that "great fat bullybag" who is even more of a pervert than her "daddy." Yes, yes, I know, that isn't "really love," because that is "unhealthy." But here we return to the mystery at the heart of the novel, or at least to an element of it, that so many people experience such "unhealthy" conditions as love—even good and essentially sane people like Dolores Haze. (One might say that what Lolita calls love at this point in her life is a particularly pitiful delusion, considering the context. But to me it not only makes sense, it shows a kind of health, *especially* given the context, that is, what she has become accustomed to. Quilty is a superior version of Humbert, a powerful adult who is giving her a great deal of attention in the form of playful conver-sation, acceptance, understanding and the promise of a better life. Remember he is an admired playwright and she encoun-ters him while acting in one of his plays; remember too that he is revealed to be impotent so that the attention she gets from him could appear to her romantic rather than purely sexual; she doesn't know about the porn movies yet.)

Nabokov famously wrote that "the initial shiver" of inspira-tion for *Lolita* came from a newspaper article he read while laid up with neuralgia; the story was about a scientist who tried to teach an ape trapped in a zoo how to draw with charcoal. The poor animal drew nothing but vertical lines—the bars of its cage. For those who distrust metaphors this anecdote may be a piece of fanciful obfuscation. But for those of us for whom metaphors are a natural way of seeing, it makes instant, terrible sense. Humbert Humbert is imprisoned in his own obsession, and so he can only and endlessly describe its most immediate manifestation: his desire for Lolita, that is, the bars of his cage—which will far more literally become the bars of her cage. This imprisonment is brilliantly specific to the characters of this specific novel. But the metaphor expands beyond the novel in relentless concentric circles: even the most well-adjusted human specimens sometimes experience a sense of imprisonment in the limitations of their bodies, culture, age, health, abilities. Now go several stops past that: what would it be like to be compelled by a desire for something you know to be grossly wrong, and to desire nothing else to the point that you are driven by it? However much one loathes pedophiles, it is hard not to feel for their predicament, for who could imagine that anyone would choose to be the way they are, despised, shunned and unable to have the basic satisfaction taken for granted by the "normal" without breaking moral and social laws that they themselves may sincerely believe in? Behind the fanatically baroque shapes of Humbert's sophistry and manic humor is an anguished human soul beating its wings against the hard, ornate construct of this persona, and which, like the starling in Humbert's poem "cannot get out."* (p. 255, *Lolita*)

Alas for the wretched starling—but in real life, a Humbert Humbert should be permanently jailed; the man who molested me should've gone to jail. There is no reasonable way to insist that anyone feel pity for such people in the courtroom or to expect that pity, if it does naturally occur in us, should result in a lenient sentence. For good or ill, I can't help but feel real-life pity for the real-life pedophile who I was unlucky enough to meet at age five. But I wish he'd been stopped when I told my mother

---

*A reference to a heart-rending segment of Laurence Sterne's *A Sentimental Journey Through France and Italy*.

about him; I wish he'd been locked up. I'm not sorry he ended his life because at least that way he didn't hurt any more children.

But the morality of art is different from the morality and justice of society, which is at least in some part practical. When Nabokov said (possibly out of sheer exasperation) that he "did not give a damn about public morals," (p. 255, *The Real Lolita*, quoting from a *Paris Review* interview) I don't believe he meant that he did not care about morality. (For anyone who has read his Lectures on Literature or even his letters, it is plain he had a strong moral sense.) I think he meant that it did not apply to his novel in the way it must apply in a court of law or any social setting. Intentionally or not, he made it possible for readers to see—or if not willing to see, then to *feel*—what his exquisitely imagined monster has in common with real and ordinary humans, and to see/sense through him that mysterious crux at the core of our existence, where the most pure and natural wishes for love, joy and union collide and become knotted with equally natural self-ishness, cruelty and wishes for crude advantage. If fiction has any moral point, it is less to give us answers or solutions than to confront us with the profound unknowability of ourselves, not just as individuals but as a species, existing in a world with a vying multitude of others. It is to remind us of the need for humility before such mystery, even when we must behave with certainty in our actions. For moral smugness is a kind of prison too, even if individuals, groups, political factions, actually entire nations might sit in it proudly—a pride that makes it seem very moral to then imprison others.

Acknowledgements

Several pieces originally appeared, in slightly different form, in the following publications:

Bookforum: "Dye Hard," "MechanicalRabbit," "She's Supposed to Make You Sick," "The Running Shadow of Your Voice" • *Elle:* "Leave the Woman Alone!" • *Harper's:* "The Trouble with Following the Rules" • *Libération:* "Worshipping the Overcoat" • SF360. org: "Beg for Your Life: On the Films of Laurel Nakadate" • *Stone Canoe:* "Somebody with a Little Hammer" • *The Village Voice:* "I've Seen It All" • *Zoetrope:* "Victims and Losers, a Love Story," "The Bridge" • *American Vogue:* "Learning to Ride"

The following pieces were previously published or collected in various works:

"A Lot of Exploding Heads," originally published in *Communion: Contemporary Writers Reveal the Bible in Their Lives*, edited by David Rosenberg (Doubleday, 1994) • "It Would Not Be Wonderful to Meet a Megalosaurus," originally published as the introduction to *Bleak House* by Charles Dickens (Modern Library,

2002) • "Remain in Light," originally published as liner notes in the three-CD album box set of *Once in a Lifetime* by Talking Heads (Rhine/Warner Bros., 2003) • "This Doughty Nose," originally published in *A New Literary History of America,* edited by Werner Sollors and Greil Marcus (Harvard University Press, 2009) • "The Easiest Thing to Forget," originally published in *Let's Talk About Love: Why Other People Have Such Bad Taste,* edited by Carl Wilson (Bloomsbury Academic, 2014) • "Icon," originally published as "Mary Gaitskill on Linda Lovelace" in *Icon,* edited by Amy Scholder (*The Feminist Press* at CUNY, 2014) • "Imaginary Light," originally published in *How to Write About Music: Excerpts from the 33 1/3 Series, Magazines, Books and Blogs with Advice from Industry-Leading Writers,* edited by Marc Woodworth and Ally-Jane Grossan (Bloomsbury Academic, an imprint of Bloomsbury Publishing Plc., 2015) • "I Cannot Get Out Said the Starling" appeared in the anthology *Lolita in the Afterlife: On Beauty, Risk, and Reckoning with the Most Indelible and Shocking Novel of the Twentieth Century,* edited by Jenny Minton Quigley (Vintage Books, 2021)

ACKNOWLEDGEMENTS

I would like to thank everyone who was a part of this in any way, particularly Jeffery Renard Allen, Jeff Parker and Mikhail Iossel. But I would especially like to thank those people who asked me to write about things it never occurred to me to write about: Knight Landesman, Greil Marcus, David Byrne, Michael Ray, Marc Woodworth, Amy Scholder, Laurel Nakadate, Carl Wilson, David Rosenberg and Jenny Minton Quigley. I also want to thank my UK editor, Hannah Westland, and my agents (in America and the UK), Jin Auh and Tracy Bohan. Most deeply I would like to thank Peter Trachtenberg and Jennifer Sears for their unfailing and intimate support.